Ideas for Art Teachers

Ideas for Art Teachers

Peter H. Gooch

B T Batsford Limited   London

© Peter H Gooch 1972
First published 1972
Reprinted 1976
ISBN 0 1734 2304 8

Filmset in Baskerville 11 on 12 point by
Filmtype Services Limited, Scarborough, Yorkshire
Printed in Great Britain by Cox & Wyman Ltd, Fakenham, Norfolk
for the publishers
B T Batsford Limited
4 Fitzhardinge Street, London W1H OAH

Contents

Acknowledgment

I should like to thank the pupils of the Bishop Thomas Grant School, Streatham, whose art work I have used to illustrate this book. My thanks are also due to Mr John Murphy, Miss Helen Casey, Mr Christopher Darton Watkins, Mr Joseph Nuttgens and other members of the art staff of the school for their helpful advice, to Mr D. Hawkins and the Commercial Photographic Service of Streatham for their considerable help with the photographs, and to my wife for typing the manuscript and for her help with research.

London 1972 PG

Introduction

This is a reference book of ideas and techniques in art suitable for use with children between the ages of 9 to 15. Most of the ideas have been illustrated with at least one photograph. The notes describing the different ideas have been kept as simple and concise as possible and have been prefixed in each case with a list of materials required to carry out the work. For those who wish for more information on particular techniques, a bibliography of art and craft books has been included at the end of this book. Naturally many ideas have had to be omitted because some are too complex to explain briefly, or are not really suitable for children, or require expensive equipment.

The material has been arranged in sections and subsections for the purpose of convenient reference, but can be used in any order or combination required by the teacher and pupil.

Examples are not meant to be copied, but are intended to encourage the pupils to discoveries and ideas of their own.

9

Composition

1 Dot and line

Pen and ink, ball point pen, felt or fibre tip pen, charcoal, pastel or paint and brush.

Several lessons can be devoted to creative work with dot and line alone. Start with exercises using dots of one size. Obtain gradations of tone by placing these close together or far apart. A link can be made with colour exercises by using dots of primary colours only. Place these beside each other so that at a distance they will appear to combine to form the secondary and tertiary colours. Make a 'pointillist' painting using dots of these three primary colours. Fibre tip pens are very suitable for this work.

Continue by using dots of varying sizes and by combining dots and freely drawn lines. Ideas may be suggested by natural forms. On the other hand non-figurative designs may eventually suggest natural forms and can then be developed into plants or creatures.

Other techniques using dots as the basic element of the design are pinholes in paper, mapping pins, nailholes in wood or tin, nail reliefs, mosaics and punched paper patterns.

Figures 1 and 2

2 Linear perspective

White paper, pencil, ruler, rubber, suitable colours.

The work should be simple and concerned with the basic fact that objects seem smaller in the distance and appear to grow larger as they approach the eye. Parallel lines appear to converge towards one another as they recede from the eye.

Examples Draw a railway line as if one were standing in the middle of the track and looking along it into the distance. This same drawing can be interpreted as a ladder or stairs or, if it is turned sideways, a fence or railings. If the parallel lines in the picture are horizontal they will meet at a vanishing point on the horizon or eye-level of the observer. This eye-level appears to rise and fall with the observer. A natural example of this is the horizon line of the sea.

10

1   *The Garden*   A fibre tip pen drawing

2   *Face*   A felt tip pen drawing

Start with simple box shapes with parallel lines converging to a single vanishing point on one eye-level. When this is mastered more complex shapes can be attempted leading to more than one eye-level and vanishing point.

Children over the age of 11 years quickly master and enjoy this work and it gives them greater confidence in their drawing. It should be stressed, however, that perspective should not be put across as the only way of drawing or painting or that all other ways are to be considered childish.

Figure 3

3 **Aerial perspective**

Pencil, ruler, scissors, cartridge paper, paint, paste.

This is an exercise illustrating the effect of water and dust in the atmosphere on the colours which reach our eyes from distant objects.

Cut from paper the outlines of rows of buildings. Paint these and paste them on top of each other onto a background paper. The foreground should be painted in strong warm colours. Add blue and grey to the colours as they appear to recede into the distance.

Figure 4

3   Linear perspective: painting in ink and wash

4   *Roofs*   An exercise in aerial perspective

4 Drawing and painting out-of-doors

Any suitable materials, portable easels and stools are useful.

Whatever the view from the art room window it is bound to be suitable as a subject for creative work even if it is only a blank wall. Of course there are always other windows in the school building which may have a more attractive outlook. In good weather work can be done in the school grounds or nearest park or trips can be made to the sea or countryside or to local churches and museums.

With younger children in particular the objects to be drawn or painted out-of-doors should be carefully chosen, otherwise a large part of the lesson may be wasted in looking for a suitable subject, or an attempt may be made to paint something beyond the child's capacities.

Figure 5

5 Drawing and painting of natural objects

As many different materials as possible with which to experiment.

Just as copying a work of art is an excellent way to appreciate it, so the making of objective drawings or paintings of natural objects is a good way to 'see' and appreciate nature. Extreme accuracy need not be stressed, especially with younger children.

Apart from developing the ability to see, drawing is essential to the creative process of projecting ideas into actuality. Creative work in any media will probably start with drawing: for instance, a lino print might be developed from an objective drawing of a flower.

Objective drawing affords an automatic link with other school subjects such as botany, biology, wood and metal craft, technical drawing and needlecraft.

14

5   View from the school window

6 Figure drawing and painting

Paper, pencil, pen, charcoal, ink, pastel or paints.

For younger children the work can be from memory. It can take the form of a self-portrait or portrait of a class-mate or member of the pupil's family, or a particular character such as a postman, butcher, policeman, etc. For older children a member of the class can pose as a model.

Emphasis on observation of the outline is important. The model can be posed in front of a strong light or against a window, the remainder of the room being kept fairly dark. The figure will then stand out as a silhouette so that the pupil can concentrate on the essential form without being distracted by unnecessary detail. Instruction should be given on how to obtain the general proportions of the figure.

7 Figure composition

Pencil, paper, paints, scissors, paste.

Several figure drawings can be combined to make a composition on a given theme, for example *a restaurant*. The pupils take turns posing for the figures in the composition. The drawings are cut out when completed and arranged and pasted onto another piece of paper, then additional objects are added to the composition such as chairs, tables, cups and saucers.

8 Shadow portraits

Pencil, white paper, paints, masking tape, artificial light.

Shadow portraits can be made on a sunny day on an outside wall. To do this in the classroom a strong light source is required such as a filmstrip projector or photographic floodlamp. Fix a large sheet of white paper to a wall with masking tape. Sit the 'model' with face in profile about one foot in front of the paper. The size of the shadow can be adjusted by moving the light and sitter in relation to the wall. Carefully outline the shadow in pencil. The sitter and the light must be absolutely still. When the drawing is finished fill in the outline with colour to make a silhouette, or draw in hairline, eyes, lips, ears, and paint the face in natural colours.

16

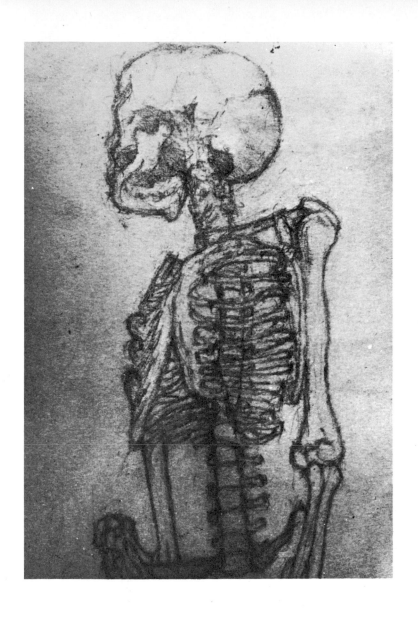

6   Pencil drawing of a skeleton by a boy of 14

9 Imaginative composition

Any suitable materials such as powder colour, poster colour, pastel.

Other subjects taught in the school can be fruitful sources of inspiration for the art lessons, eg

Religion   The Old and New Testaments contain a wealth of dramatic stories suitable for all sorts of creative work, eg The Creation, The Flood, Jonah and the Whale, The Tower of Babel, The Plagues of Egypt, Crossing the Red Sea, The Nativity, The Flight into Egypt, The Last Supper, The Resurrection.

English   Every sort of literature is rich in ideas for the artist. Fairy tales, adventure stories, myths and legends, poetry, humorous verse, ballads, detective stories, novels. Good examples are *The Wind in the Willows, Alice in Wonderland, Grimm's Fairy Tales, Moby Dick, Three Men in a Boat, Gulliver's Travels. 20,000 Leagues Under the Sea, The War of the Worlds, Oliver Twist, Macbeth.*

Music   The music played in the art class should have plenty of contrast and suggest many different moods. The children should listen until an idea is suggested by the music, but should not feel obliged to do something because the teacher expects it.

Figures 7 and 8

7   A painting created whilst listening to a record

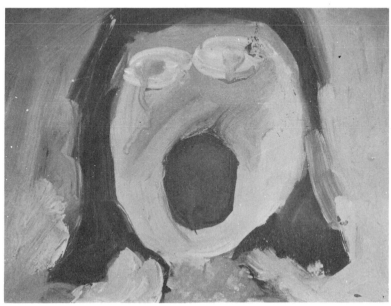

8   *Fear*   Painting on an abstract theme

10 Abstract themes

Any suitable materials.

Imaginative composition can also include general themes, not only particular subjects such as those suggested in section nine. These demand more of the imagination and are more suitable for older children. For example, instead of *The Forest in Winter* the subject might be *Cold*. These can be treated figuratively or symbolically in colours and shapes alone. Some generalized ideas to use are: fear, anger, peace, youth, speed, rebellion, freedom, force, evil, happiness, energy, vanity, strength, pain, shame, justice, faith, and death.

11 Doodling

Sugar paper, charcoal, paints or any other suitable materials.

Doodling, like blot-making, can be an aid to the imagination. Scribble freely over a large sheet of paper. The shapes drawn may be as varied as possible. There should be no attempt to execute any preconceived idea. When the paper is completely covered with lines, look for meaningful shapes. If the first attempt fails, turn the paper round and add more scribble. When some significant shapes are found, emphasize these with a thicker line of charcoal or paint. The lines which are not required can be rubbed out or painted over and the work completed in any material.

Figure 9

9   Doodling: an Octopus

12 Line blowing

Thin paints or inks, drinking straw, paper.

Dip the end of a drinking straw into the colour and drop a blot from it onto the paper. Use the straw to blow the ink about the paper and form a pattern with it. With a little practice firm control can be exercised over the design.

To avoid chaotic results the pupil must have a clear intention before commencing. The completed work will then be the instructive result of conflict between intention and accidental effect.

Figures 10 and 11

10   *Girl*   Line blowing, ink on paper

11 *Spiders* Coloured waterproof inks blown over the paper:
the paper was soaked under a tap before the ink was dry

13 Finger painting

Smooth non-absorbent paper or foil, powder paint, paste.

Mix the paint and paste together to form a liquid of creamy consistency. Pour this onto the paper and spread it out. Draw freely into this with the fingers working quickly before the paint dries.

Figures 12 and 13

12   *Coils*   Finger painting

13 *Fir Trees* Finger painting made by drawing the fingernail
through the paint

14 **Wet into wet**

Inks, poster or powder paints, strong absorbent paper, pen or brush, sponge, drawing board.

Wet the paper on both sides under a running tap. Put the paper onto a wet drawing board. Sponge away any large puddles of water as these may cause the colours to become completely out of control. Draw quickly with pen or brush over the damp surface. If the paper dries too quickly, re-dampen it with a sponge.

Waterproof inks have a peculiar quality of their own, but once dry they cannot be affected by adding more water.

Figures 14 and 15

14   Pen and watercolour ink drawing on wet paper

15 *Tree* Wet into wet painting using waterproof inks on grey
sugar paper

15 Wax crayon and turpentine

Wax crayons, paper, turpentine substitute, brush.

Make a bold composition using coloured wax crayons. Paint into this with a brush dipped in turpentine substitute. This will cause the wax to dissolve and blur giving a rich oil-painterly effect.

16 Smoke painting

Candle, white card, fixative.

Hold a piece of card horizontally over a candle flame. Move the candle quickly to and fro so that the carbon from the candle forms an image. Alterations are possible by scratching or rubbing the carbon. Additions can be made in other materials, and the work made permanent by using a fixative.

Figures 16 and 17

16 *Dog* Smoke painting

17   *Face*   Smoke painting

17 Blot making

Ink or paint, brush, paper.

Splash paint or ink onto a piece of paper. Fold the paper in half quickly and press it together. When opened out, the blots of ink will have formed themselves into a symmetrical shape. This shape may suggest an idea such as a face, which can be developed by adding more paint.

Figures 18 and 19

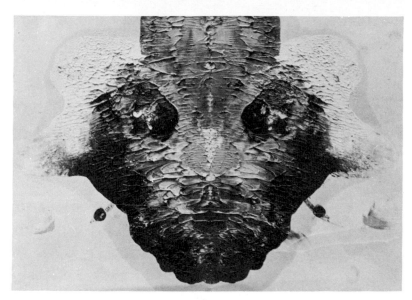

18   Blot painting using oil paint: an interesting veined texture is achieved when the two halves of the paper are separated

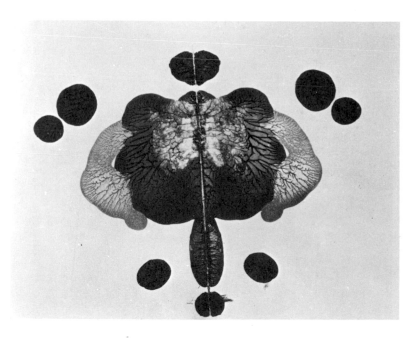

19   Blot painting

18 Copying works of art

Any suitable materials.

An excellent way to appreciate a work of art is to copy it from the original if possible or, if not convenient, from a good reproduction. The work should be freely copied and may be translated from one medium to another. It would be natural to link this work to a study of the history and appreciation of art.

Figure 20

20   A linocut copy of a lithograph by Charles Munch

19   Large communal painting

Large background sheet of paper or cloth. Sheets of sugar paper. *Sellotape (Scotch Tape)*, scissors, paste, paints, brushes.

The background materials must be strong. If paper is used several sheets can be joined together with *Sellotape* to make one larger sheet. Place the background on a large table or group of tables, or put it on the floor. Each child draws and paints separate items. These are cut out and pasted onto the large background in the appropriate places. When all the sections are completed and stuck on, additions can be made with a paintbrush. Before the work is complete it should be fixed in place so that it can be viewed at a distance and alterations and/or additions made.

   This method is suitable for painting large areas such as may be required for stage scenery or Christmas decorations.

Figures 21 and 22

21   Large communal painting of a country town

22 *Ban the Bomb* Detail of a mural executed as described in section 19

Pattern

20 Dot and line pattern

Pen and ink, fibre or felt tip pen.

As suggested in section one, pattern work can be done using dots and lines only. The two basic elements in design, unity and variety, are achieved by using these simple shapes over and over again. By making them large or small, close together or far apart, an immense variety can be achieved. Fibre tip pens are particularly suited to this work. Their precision and bright colours are very pleasing to children.

Figure 23

23   Dot and line pattern made with fibre tip pen

21 Colour exercises

Pencil, paper, paints, coloured papers, scissors, paste.

Carry out various exercises in mixing and gradating tones and colours. For example:

(a) In figure 24 the inspiration for this was a discussion in the classroom on the similarity between natural forms such as rock strata, wood grain, the skin of an onion, and the flow of water. A drawing was then made and painted in colours graded from blue through green, yellow, orange and red to purple.

(b) Find objects of a two-dimensional nature with an interesting outline. Make a design by drawing round these on the paper so that the shapes overlap each other. Imagine that each object is transparent and of a primary colour so that where they overlap they will produce the secondary colours. Colour in accordingly.

(c) Divide the paper with criss-cross lines. Choose a dominant key colour. Use this colour throughout the design, but with a small addition of some other colour in each space.

(d) Squares: this exercise demonstrates our subjective reactions to colours. The middle square in each case in figure 25 is cut from a sheet of paper of the same colour. The surrounding squares are each of a different colour. When complete, the central squares will appear to differ in colour and shade from each other.

Figures 24 and 25

24 Exercise in colour gradation. As the final effect suggested the sun over the sea some crabs and a ship were added later

25 Coloured squares

22 Combed pattern

Inks, powder paint mixed with paste, plastic paint or poster paint, brush, scissors, card, paper.

Cardboard looms designed for simple weaving make good combs for this work, but any piece of thick cardboard will do. Cut V-shaped teeth with the points about 6 mm ($\frac{1}{4}$ in.) apart along one edge. The card should be large enough to fit comfortably into the hand. Dip the toothed edge in paint and drag it across the paper to make a design, or put thick paint on the paper first, then drag the comb through it.

Figure 26

23 Action painting

Any paints (turpentine substitute for oil paint), paper or hardboard, rag, newspaper.

The best way to do this is to have a large clear floor area covered with plenty of newspaper. For dribbling and trickling, a viscous paint is required such as ordinary house paint, which will fall easily from the brush or straight out of the tin. The painting should be done on large sheets of paper or on hardboard. Other paints, powder, poster, plastic or oil, can be splashed, flicked, sprayed, trickled and blown; or can even be printed with the palms of the hands or the soles of the feet. Dry paint, sand or plaster can be sprinkled into the wet paint. Have plenty of rag and turpentine or water ready for cleaning up. The pupils should be well covered. The ideal protective garment for this is a boiler suit.

Figure 27

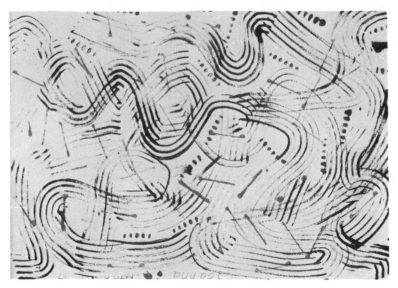

26　Combed pattern

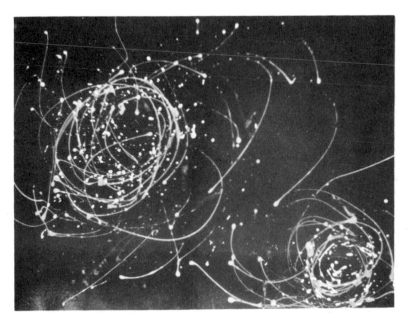

27　Action painting: house paint on hardboard dripped from a large brush with rhythmic arm movements

24 Sand painting

Adhesive, brush, cardboard box lid, sand, sawdust, stonedust, brickdust, glitter, iron filings, gold, silver or bronze powder.

Large cardboard box lids are useful because they help to contain the sand, but sheets of card or paper will do. Paint the shapes in with a brush which has been dipped in adhesive. Glue one area at a time, and scatter the sand quickly so that it sticks before the glue starts to dry, then pour the surplus material back into its receptacle.

Sand can be coloured by mixing it with ink or dye; then spread it out to dry on a plaster slab in a warm place. Keep the colours in separate receptacles.

Figures 28 and 29

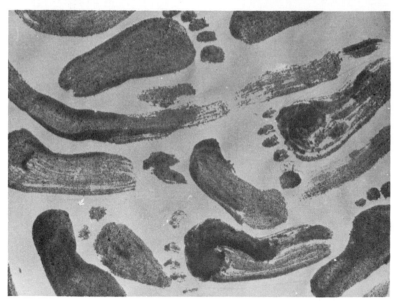

28 *Footsteps* Sand painting painted with PVA emulsion then sprinkled with sand

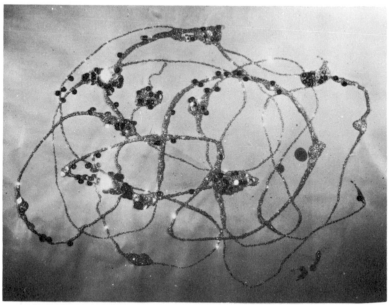

29 This design was made by trickling adhesive direct from the bottle. Then glitter and sequins were scattered over the surface

25 Marbling

Sink or large bowl or photographic dish. Oil paint or oil based inks, turpentine substitute, cartridge paper.

This technique was traditionally used for the edges of pages and the end papers of books. Any oil based paint or ink can be used. This must be thinned with turpentine substitute so that it will float on the surface of the water. Marbling inks can be bought ready for use. A large receptacle is required to contain the water. The paper is dipped vertically into, or placed on the surface of the water, so that it will pick up the marbling when it is removed. Single or combined colours can be used. Other materials or objects can be decorated in this way such as eggs or balloons. The natural propensity for oil and water to repel each other can cause the colour to spread further than intended, therefore great control is required with this technique.

A marbling effect can also be obtained by pouring various thin coloured oil paints or house paints onto card and allowing them to run into each other.

Figures 30 and 31

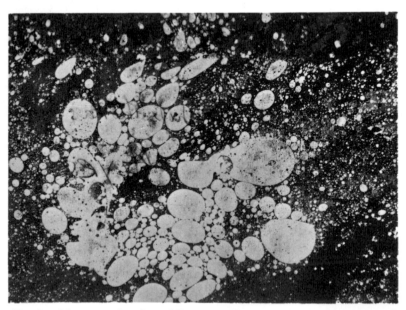

30 In this example of marbling paraffin was mixed with coloured inks and then poured onto the surface of the water

31 Marbling: the bird was cut from a magazine and pasted on
when the marbling was dry

26 Wheel patterns

Paper, inks, powder paint or poster paint, brush, pottery wheel.

The paper must not be much bigger than the pottery wheel. Wet the underside of the paper so that it adheres to the wheel. Colours can be splashed or brushed on as the wheel revolves. A wet into wet effect is obtained by soaking both sides of the paper. The designs of course will always be circular in shape. These can be cut out when dry and combined to form larger compositions.

Figure 32

32   Patterns formed on a pottery wheel using thin powder colours

27 Geometric designs

Ruler, compass, pencil, pen, inks or paint, plain or graph paper, small brush.

Experiment with ruler and compass. See what designs can be made with straight lines only and with circles only. Use graph paper to obtain fixed points from which a compass can be used. It is better to doodle with the compass and ruler until an interesting pattern emerges rather than to have some preconceived idea which will probably not be effective when put down on paper.

Figures 33, 34 and 35

33   A geometric pattern made with pen and ink

34   Geometric pattern using curved lines only

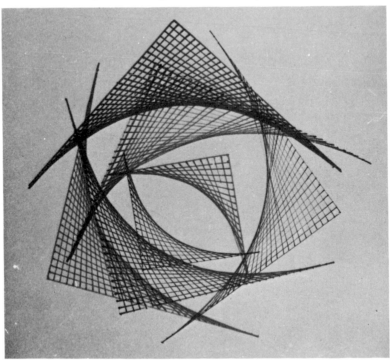

35   Curve stitch composition: felt pens on sugar paper

28 Curve stitching

Pencil, compass, ruler, needle, thin card, *Sellotape* (*Scotch Tape*), thread.

Use card and thread of contrasting colours. Plan the design on the card with compass and ruler. Mark off the edges of the shapes with equally spaced dots. Prick through each dot with a needle. Thread the needle and knot the end of the thread. Start from behind the card and sew from point to point on the design. Complete the sewing behind the card and stick the end of the thread down with a piece of *Sellotape*.

Here are some basic curve stitching shapes:

Angles   Draw an angle with pencil and ruler. Divide up both lines into equal parts using small dots. Number the dots on one line 1 2 3 4 and so on from the outside inwards. Number the other line in the same way, but starting at one dot from the middle and going outwards. Join the dots 1 to 1, 2 to 2, 3 to 3 and so on with straight lines.

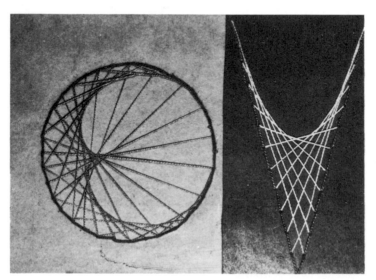

36a Curve stitch designs made with wool thread through coloured cards

48

Circle Divide the circumference of a circle into 48 parts. Number each quarter of the circle from 1 to 12. Join all the 1's together with a straight line. Do the same with the 2s, 3s and so on.

Heart shape Make a circle and divide it into 36 parts. Number the dots from 1 to 36. Join 1 to 2, 2 to 4, 3 to 6, 4 to 8 and so on.

Kidney shape Make a circle and number it as above. This time join 1 to 3, 2 to 6, 3 to 9, 4 to 12.

Make other geometric patterns by sewing through card. These, of course, can only be made up of straight lines.

Figures 36a and 36b

36b Curve stitch designs made with wool thread through coloured card

29 Thread patterns

Thick wood board, large-headed nails or map pins, hammer, pliers, coloured threads, string, wire, or elastic bands, scissors, paint or coloured paper.

The wood can be stained and polished or painted, or can have coloured paper attached to it. The nails or pins can be arranged geometrically or irregularly. For regular designs graph paper or ruler and compass can be used. The threads should be of contrasting colour to the background and are wound from nail to nail without tying. To start or finish off, simply wind the thread around a nailhead several times.

Figure 37

30 Paper weaving

Papers of contrasting colours, scissors, craft knife, pencil, ruler.

To make a paper mat fold a sheet of paper in half. With the fold at the bottom, cut vertical slits at equal intervals to within about a finger's width of the top. Open the paper out. Take another sheet of paper of the same size but in a contrasting colour. Divide this up into strips, and weave these through the slits in the first paper. The pattern can be varied by using mixed coloured papers, varying the widths of the strips, or by weaving over or under more than one strip at a time. The slits and strips can be curved, zigzag, or cut diagonally. For asymmetrical designs do not fold the paper but place it flat on a board and cut the slits with a craft knife.

In addition to paper, or as a substitute, weave in string, wool thread, pipe cleaners, cane, raffia, ribbons or tape. The overall shape of the paper need not be rectangular. It can be irregular or even figurative.

Figure 38

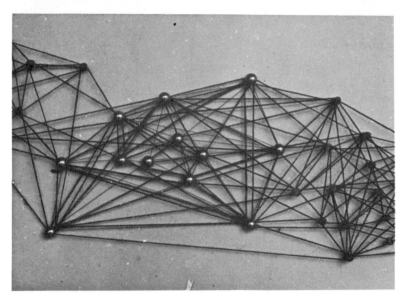

37   This thread pattern was made with upholsterers' tacks and tintacks. The idea was to have the thread running from each nail to all other nails on the board

38   Paper weaving: curved strips give an 'op art' effect

31   Easter egg decoration

Eggs, eggcup or small jar, any suitable materials.

Boil the egg beforehand to reduce the risk of breakage. Put the egg in an eggcup or similar receptacle. This helps to avoid smudging the design with the fingers and also prevents the egg rolling onto the floor.

Almost any technique which can be used on paper can also be used on the eggshell: drawing with pen and ink, felt pens, painting with oil or water based colours, dyeing, wax resist, stencilling, marbling, ink blowing, collage, wax scratching.

Figure 39

39   Decorated eggs

Engraving

32 Scraperboard

Scraperboard, pen, brush, indian ink, stencil knife, craft knife or penknife.

Scraperboard consists of a card with a thin coating of white clay over the surface on one side. It can be obtained with an already blackened surface or with a white surface to which ink can be added. White lines and areas are obtained by scratching through the top layer of black ink with a sharp instrument such as a linocutting tool, craft knife, compass point. The white surface offers more creative opportunity because coloured inks and paints can be used as well as black, and a considerable amount of drawing can be done before using the scraper. The ink or paint must be absolutely dry before scraping commences.

Scraperboards can also be obtained with various stippled surfaces.

Figure 40

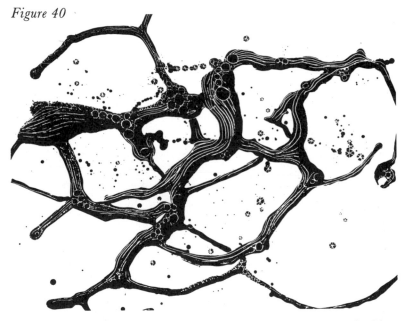

40   In this example ink was dribbled onto the surface of white scraperboard and the card was tilted to make the ink run in different directions. When dry the ink was scratched with a craft knife

33 Engraving on black card

Card, paint, sewing needle.

The surface of black card can be scratched with a needle so that the white card beneath shows through, or card can be darkened with paint and then scratched when dry. The paint should be applied thickly with not too much water so that it does not soak into the surface of the card.

34 Engraving on plaster

Plaster, bowl, cardboard lid, paint or ink, brush, sewing needle.

Make a plaster slab by pouring plaster into a cardboard lid. When it has set, paint the plaster with a dark coloured ink or paint. When the colour is dry, scratch a design through the paint with a needle so that the white plaster shows through.

It is possible to use this slab as a printing surface. Ink the surface of the plaster as if it were a linocut and print in the usual way.

35 Wax engraving

Wax crayons, craft knife or penknife, cartridge paper, newspaper.

Cover the table top with newspaper because the small pieces of wax spread about and are difficult to remove. Using a light coloured wax crayon, rub a thick layer of wax over the cartridge paper. (Thin paper should not be used as it is easy to rub or cut through it by accident.) Over the first wax layer, rub on another of a darker colour. Black is the most effective colour because it gives the greatest contrast. Scrape a design through the top layer to reveal the colour beneath.

Figure 41

41 Wax engraving

36 **Paint engraving**

Any thick paint, sugar or cartridge paper, brush, old paintings.

Use either old paintings which would be thrown away or paint a sheet of paper with different colours. Light colours are best. When the paint is thoroughly dry, put a thick layer of black paint over it. While this is still wet, scratch a design with the point of the handle of a brush through the black paint.

Resist

37 Wax crayon resist

Colourless wax candles or white wax crayons, poster, powder paints or inks, white paper, brush.

Draw the design with wax crayons or with a candle onto white paper. Paint lightly over the wax with a brush loaded with ink or thin paint. The waxed areas will resist the colour and remain white while the non-waxed areas will absorb the colour. When dry, further wax can be added and another wash of a darker colour brushed on.

Figure 42

38 Dripped wax resist

Colourless wax candle, white card, inks, poster or powder paint, brush.

Card is used because the background must be rigid when held in one hand while the other hand holds a lighted candle. Hold the card almost vertical to obtain long splashes of wax. Turn the card to vary the design. Put on colours as described in section 37.

Figure 43

39 Melted wax resist on paper or cloth

Paraffin wax, double boiler, brush, fixative mouth spray (or old toothbrush or scrubbing brush and knife), ink or cold water dyes, paper or cloth, bowl, flat iron, rubber gloves, newspaper.

For wax resist on paper, melt paraffin wax or candle ends in a double boiler or in a tin can in a saucepan of water. Keep the wax warm while in use. Apply the wax with a brush or by splashing. Spray ink or thin paint over the wax with a fixative mouth spray or splatter with a brush and knife.

For wax resist on cloth (batik) melt the wax (as described above), place the cloth on a newspaper or stretch and tack it over a frame. Paint the wax design on both sides of the cloth.

56

42   Wax crayon resist

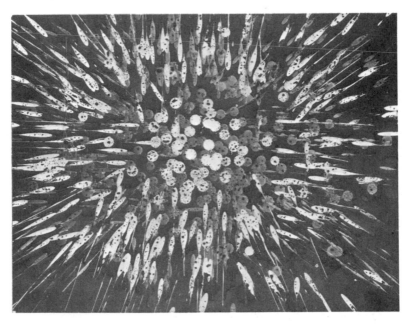

43   Dripped wax resist on card

Immerse the cloth in a cold water dye, then remove it from the dye and hang it up to dry. If a second colour is desired, add more wax over the dyed parts of the cloth and then dye again with a darker colour. The wax can be ironed out of the cloth between several sheets of paper or melted out in hot water. If it is melted out in a sink, take care that the wax does not go down the sink outlet because it will block it.

The well-known batik crackle effect is produced by the dye penetrating through cracks in the wax to the cloth beneath. If this is not desired, use beeswax, which is less brittle. If an exaggerated crackle effect is wanted, use paraffin wax and squeeze the cloth in the hands before dyeing.

Batik designs can also be made by wax rubbing. The cloth is stretched tight on a frame. Put the frame cloth side down over the area to be rubbed and wax it evenly with a candle or crayon, then dye in the usual way.

Figures 44 and 45

44   Wax pattern applied by splashing. Ink was sprayed over the wax with a fixative mouth spray

45 Wax resist on cloth (batik)

40 Tie and dye

String, elastic band, scissors, cloth, dye, bowl, rubber gloves.

This is a method of resist dyeing using string or elastic bands to prevent the dye penetrating to the cloth.

Binding Pull the cloth into a point wherever a circular shape is required. Tie thread around the point, then bind closely and tightly along the cloth. The size of the circle will depend on the length of the binding. Continue by binding back to the beginning, then tie off. Elastic bands twisted tightly around the cloth give a slightly different effect. If the cloth is dyed with cold water dye, waxed string may be used or the string can be waxed before dyeing to help prevent penetration. After tying, immerse the cloth in the dye, following the manufacturer's instructions carefully. When dry, add more string to the cloth, then re-dye in a darker colour. Do not remove any string until the cloth is completely dry.

Twisting and coiling method Twist the cloth into a rope-like shape, tie both ends with a string, continue twisting until the cloth begins to coil back on itself, then fold cloth in half and tie the two ends together. Bind tightly along the entire length of the doubled-over cloth. Dye in the usual way. When dry, further binding may be added, and a second colour dyed, or the two ends of the coil may be dyed in different colours.

Marbling method Squeeze the cloth into a ball and twist string tightly around it in all directions. Tie off, but leave a long piece of string which can be held in the hand to dip the ball into the dye bath. Allow the cloth to dry before untying the string. Rearrange the cloth, re-tie and dye again in another colour. When the dyeing is completed, untie and iron the cloth while it is still damp.

Patterns on cloth can also be made by painting, dripping and splashing the dye.

Figures 46 and 47

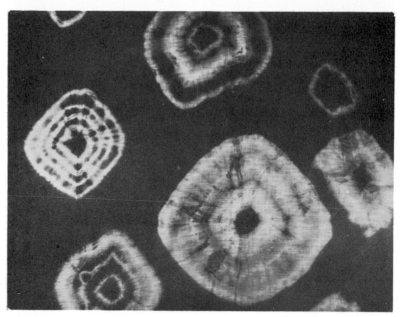

46 Example of tie and dye: the binding was done with string and elastic bands

47 Cloth tied in the various ways before dyeing described in section 40

Print making

The various methods of reproduction outlined below, apart from being another area of exploration, deal with techniques for repeating images many times. This means that complex designs can be built up from simple beginnings with comparative ease and speed.

Objects with which printed patterns can be made are almost infinite. The materials used in the page of prints illustrated in figure 48 are a rubber eraser cut to a triangular shape, a fingerprint, a button, the end of a cotton reel, string, the end of a matchbox. Other materials from which prints can be taken are impressed plasticine or clay, corrugated cardboard, coarse cloth or sacking, patterned glass, crumpled paper, the grain of wood, wire netting, machine parts, nail and screw heads, leaves, feathers, bark.

Figures 48 and 49

48   A page of prints from various materials

49 *Head* Designs can be made by using the inking roller itself
direct onto the paper

41 Stick printing

Ink or paint, printing sticks, the end of a straw, thin dowel rod or end of a paintbrush handle.

Special hardwood printing sticks can be bought cut to a variety of shapes, but the end of any stick-like object can be used to print with.

Figures 50 and 51

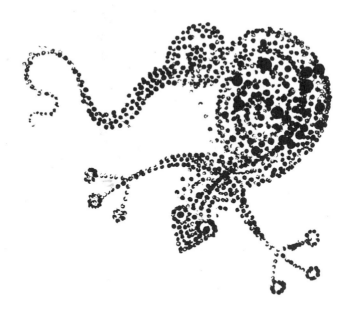

50 *Lizard* Made by dipping the end of a paintbrush handle in printing ink. The larger dots were made with hardwood printing sticks

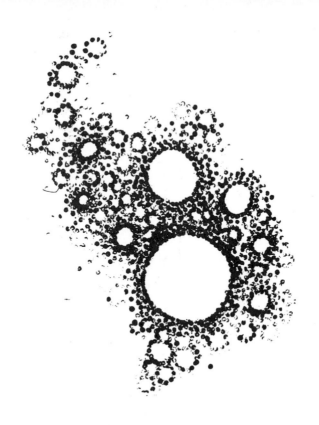

51   A drinking straw was dipped in paint to produce this design

42 Card edge print

Various thicknesses of card can be used, scissors, paper, ink or paint, ink pad or brush.

Use rectangular pieces of card that can be held comfortably in the hand. Paint the edge of the card with the brush or use an inking pad. This pad can be made by sticking felt or foam rubber into a tin lid or saucer. Print the design by pressing the wet edge of the card onto an absorbent paper. Experiment with different lengths and thicknesses of card.

Figures 52 and 53

52   *Portrait*   Card edge print

53 *Seeds* Ink was splattered over this design after printing with a card edge

43 String print

Card, scissors, strong glue, craft knife, string, or wire, ink plate, printing rollers, printing ink, absorbent paper.

String can be used as a printing surface by sticking it to thick card with a strong adhesive. The string must be of one thickness. Also, if it crosses over itself, it must be cut and reset, otherwise the printing surface will be uneven and will not print clearly.

When the glue is dry the string is inked up with a roller. The paper is placed over the block and a clean roller or the back of a spoon is passed over the paper.

Figure 54

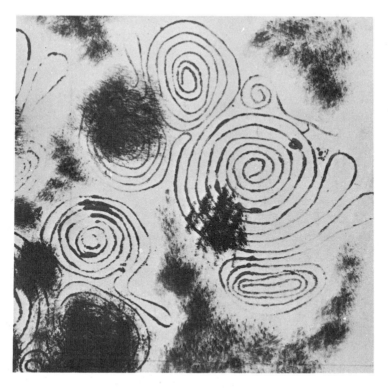

54   String print: paint was added afterwards with a stencil brush. The same block was used to make a wax resist rubbing as in figure 71

44   String printing from a cylinder

String, cardboard tube, jam jar, bottle, tin-can or other cylindrical object, strong adhesive, ink or paint, paper, inking plate, brush.

Brush glue over the surface of the cylinder. Wind the string around it, making sure that it is firmly attached, particularly at the ends. Leave a space at the ends of the cylinder for the hands so that the tube can be rolled comfortably. When the glue is dry, ink or paint the string and roll it in different directions over the paper.

Figure 55

55   String print from a cylinder

45 Printing drawn string

String or thread, ink or paint, paper, drawing board.

Soak the thread or string in ink or paint and drop it onto a sheet of paper. Put another sheet of paper on top of it and put a drawing board on top of this. Pull the thread in different directions while drawing it out.

Figure 56

46 Crumpled paper print

Cartridge paper, ink plate, printing rollers, printing ink, iron.

Crumple up a thick sheet of paper, ink over the creased surface with a roller. When the ink is dry, iron out the creases.

47 Wood grain print

Ink plate, printing rollers, printing ink, kitchen paper.

Search for old pieces of wood with an interesting surface texture—knots, holes, and prominent grain. The grain can be accentuated by prolonged soaking in water or by brushing with a stiff wire brush. Dry the wood thoroughly, ink up the surface and print in the usual way.

48 Paper print

Cartridge paper, scissors, craft knife, adhesive, printing ink, inking plate, rollers.

Cut or tear out paper shapes and arrange and stick them onto a larger sheet of paper or card. Ink up the entire sheet and print in the usual way from it.

56 A drawn thread print

49 Printing from PVA emulsion

PVA emulsion (*Gloy, Marvin Medium*), brush, paper or card, and the usual printing materials.

Paint a design with PVA emulsion on card or paper. Allow it to dry thoroughly, then ink up the surface of the emulsion and print as usual. Other materials which can be printed in this way when dry are plaster of paris, alabastine and *Polyfilla*.

Figure 57

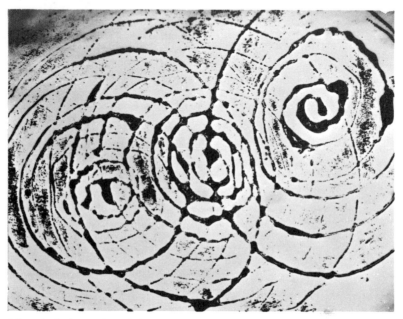

57   A design printed from PVA emulsion by trickling it direct from the container

50 Cut card print

Thin card or cartridge paper, kitchen paper, rollers, ink, inking plate, scissors, craft knife, newspaper.

Cut the shape required from the card or cartridge paper. Place it on a sheet of newspaper and ink it up with a roller. Place the cut out shape face upwards onto another piece of paper. Put the kitchen paper over it and roll over the back of the paper with a clean roller.

Figures 58 and 59

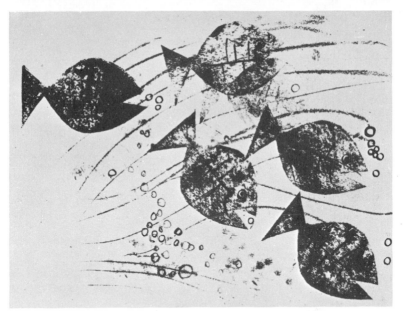

58 *Fish* After the cut card was printed lines and bubbles were added by monoprinting

59 *Girl* Cut card print. The first card was a cut-out of the face and hair and was printed in brown ink. The second card was a cut-out of the hair alone and was printed black

51 Monoprinting

Printing ink, roller, printing plate, newsprint or kitchen paper, a pointed tool such as the end of a brush handle, ball point pen or matchstick.

Roll out ink or paint evenly over the inking plate. This plate can be of any non-absorbent material such as glass, plastic, lino, metal, or the surface of a formica top table. Place a sheet of kitchen paper over the ink and draw on the paper with a pointed object. Areas of soft shading can be made by rubbing with the fingertips. Peel off the paper and the drawing will be found on the underside in reverse.

    To make a negative print, do not add any more ink to the plate. Place another thin sheet of paper over the plate and rub over the back. Peel off the paper and a negative of the previous print will be found on the other side.

    For direct monoprinting, ink up the plate as before, but draw directly into the ink with a pointed object or with the finger, then put the paper over the ink and rub over the back.

Figures 60 and 61

52 Masked monoprint

Printing ink, roller, printing plate, newsprint or kitchen paper, scissors.

After putting ink on the inking plate and rolling it out evenly, place cut or torn paper shapes onto the plate. These will act as a mask and appear as white shapes on a dark background when the paper is pressed over the ink.

74

60   *Dove*   A monoprint

61   Positive and negative monoprints from the same inking-plate

53 Potato cut

Potato, penknife, craft knife or lino tool, paper, paintbrush or ink pad, water paint or water based printing ink.

Cut the potato in half. Cut a simple design on the face of the potato. Complicated designs are not necessary. Very simple shapes can be effective when combined and repeated in an interesting way. Put the paint on the printing surface with a brush or press the potato into an ink pad.

Potato prints can be successfully combined with other techniques on cloth such as tie and dye or batik using fabric printing colours.

Figure 62

54 Progressive linocut

Lino, lino-cutting tools, printing ink, inking plate, rollers, paper, rag.

This method is also called waste or reduction lino-cutting. Cut out parts of the lino which are required to print white. Make as many prints as required using one colour. Clean the lino and remove further parts of the design with the lino-cutter. Print the lino in a different colour on top of the first set of prints so that what has been cut away the second time will leave the first colour showing through. Continue in this way by removing more lino and printing over the previous prints until the lino is almost entirely cut away.

62 Potato cut print on paper. The surface of the potato was cut
with a craft knife. The centre of the motif was made by pushing a pen
nib holder through the middle of the potato

55 Linocut

Linoleum (ordinary floor linoleum can be used and can be obtained as offcuts from shops and building sites). Linocutting tools, ink, inking plate, roller, absorbent paper, rag.

Practice first by cutting direct designs based on the natural shapes made by the linocutting tools. If a light coloured lino is used, the surface can be painted black. The parts removed by the cutters will then appear light against a dark background as in the final print. When cutting, keep the hand holding the lino behind the cutting tool. The inks can be water or oil based. Water based inks are cleaner to use, but oil based inks are more transparent and give more subtle effects.

63   A linocut print based on a magazine photograph simplified into basic light and dark areas and double-printed in two colours. This gives a three dimensional effect or impression of movement

When printing, put the paper over the face of the inked up lino, run a clean roller over the back of the paper or rub it with a spoon. If the lino is weakened by cutting, it can be mounted on a wood block cut to size. It will have to be mounted on wood (type high) for combining with letterpress printing.

Figures 63 and 64

64   *Bishop*   Linocut based on a brass rubbing mounted type-high on a wood block combined with type and printed on a letterpress machine

56 Rotation linocut printing

Lino, lino-cutting tools, printing ink, inking plate, rollers, paper, rag.

Cut an abstract design on a square piece of lino. Print it out as many times as desired in one colour, then clean the lino and ink it up with a different colour. Turn the lino 45° and set it accurately on top of the first prints and print it again. Repeat this process using two more colours and turning the lino each time. This can make a very effective all-over print suitable for a fabric design.

57 Linocut print on fabric

Linocut mounted on a wood block, fabric, fabric printing colours, roller and ink plate or felt pad, large piece of felt or blanket or newspapers, hammer, large table.

The linocut must be mounted on a piece of wood the same size as itself. This should be at least a half inch thick. Glue it on the wood with a strong adhesive. The lino can be inked with a roller or pressed face down onto an inking pad. Fix the cloth over a large sheet of felt, blanket or newspapers. Position the inked block face downwards on the cloth and tap the back with a hammer.

Figure 65

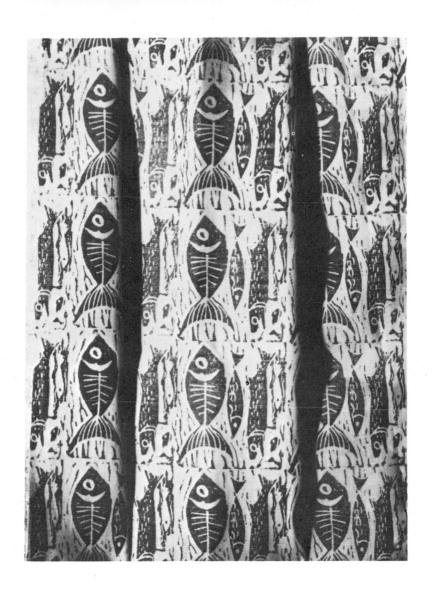

65 *Fish* Linocut on cloth. The pieces of lino left sticking up
between the main masses help to unite the design

58 Screen printing

Printing frame, cotton organdie, squeegee, powder paint mixed with water paste or screen printing colours, kitchen paper or newspapers, cartridge paper, gumstrip paper, craft knife or stencil knife, staple gun.

Stretch the organdie over one side of the frame and tack it down with staples around the edge. It must be drum-tight. It can be made tighter by first wetting it under a tap. Soak gumstrip paper in water and mask the outside of the screen. Make sure that the strips are stuck firmly over the edge of the frame so the paint cannot seep through. Put the prepared paper stencil onto the surface to be printed. This stencil can be cut out with a knife, but a very simple stencil can be made by tearing up strips of paper and arranging them into a design. Place the screen (cloth-side down) over the stencil paper. Pour the paint into the screen at one end, then squeegee it across to the other end.

Apart from paper other materials which can be used to act as stencils are wax, lacquer, rubber solution, oil paint, glue. Wax is particularly suitable as it dries quickly and is easily removed by ironing between sheets of paper.

Prints like these can make excellent materials for skirts, blouses, curtains, cushion covers, etc.

Figures 66 and 67

66   Screen print on paper. The stencils were made from fold and cut paper designs. Two different coloured paints were squeegeed at the same time

67   Screen print on cloth. Helizarin colours using a stencil of torn paper strips

59 Leaf printing

Leaves, ink, rollers, inking plate, paper.

Among the many varied materials which can be printed, leaves are probably the most exciting. Using a roller, ink the leaf lengthways, taking care that it does not wrap itself around the roller. Place a sheet of paper over the leaf, then roll over the back of the paper with a clean roller.

In illustration 68, leaf printing has been incorporated into a school magazine in a collection of poems called *Autumn*. This was printed on a *Gestetner* litho machine. The leaves were inked with an oil-based ink and pressed onto paper litho plates. A separate plate was made for each colour and for the typed poems.

Plates are available from *Gestetner*. The thin plates run off up to 50 copies and the better quality plates can duplicate into thousands.

Figure 68

60 Paper lithography

Ensink litho sketch paper, litho sketch ink, litho sketch solution, litho crayon, soft cloth or cotton wool, rubber eraser, inking rollers or spoon, inking plate, cartridge paper.

Orthodox lithography is a difficult medium to use in the class-room because it requires cumbersome and expensive equipment. With the development of paper litho, the technique has become simple enough even for very young children to use.

As with traditional litho, the process depends upon the greasy part of the plate taking the ink which is applied to it while the non-greasy parts repel the ink.

Draw with litho chalk upon the white side of the litho paper. Wet the entire surface of the paper by dabbing with a piece of soft cloth or cotton wool which has been soaked in the special litho solution. Ink up the roller with litho printing ink, and roll this over the damped printing surface. Place a sheet of cartridge paper over the inked up plate and run a clean roller over the back of the paper or rub with the back of a spoon. It will probably take several prints before a satisfactory one is obtained. The paper must be re-damped with the solution and re-inked before taking each print. Rest the hand on a spare piece of paper so that greasy fingermarks are not made

68　Leaf print on a litho plate

on the paper plate. Unwanted marks can be removed with a firm rubber eraser.

If more than one colour is required, a separate plate must be used to print each colour. Registration will not be difficult providing each paper plate is cut to the same size.

Rubbing

61 Rub-through print

Kitchen paper, wax crayons or heel-ball, thin card or heavy cartridge paper, scissors, craft knife.

Draw a shape on the card or cartridge paper, cut it out, place the shape beneath a sheet of kitchen paper. Feel for the shape with the fingers, then rub over it with the crayon, concentrating particularly on the edge. Move the shape under the paper and rub again to produce a repetitive image.

Some other surfaces which can be rubbed through are string, wire, ribbed glass, corrugated cardboard, bark, brickwork, wire mesh, grain of wood, woodblock flooring, leaves, pressed flowers, feathers.

Figure 69

69 *Bottles and glasses* Rub-through print. Three pieces of card were
used, one for the bottle, one for the label and one for the glass

62 Rub-through print using old linocuts

Kitchen paper, coloured wax crayons, old linocuts.

Good linocuts should not be thrown away. In figure 70 two separate linocuts have been combined to make this imaginative composition. The linocuts were placed beneath the paper and were rubbed through with a wax crayon in the manner of a brass rubbing. By moving the linos about under the paper a number of repeated images were created.

Figure 70

70   Rub through print using old linocuts

63 Wax resist rubbing

Candles or white wax crayons, water based paint, brush, kitchen paper.

Wax crayons or candles can be used for rubbing as described above. Then put a thin watercolour wash over the paper and the wax will resist the paint.

Figure 71

71   Wax resist rubbing over a string block

64 Brass rubbing

A roll of lining or detail paper, masking tape, scissors, heel-ball or wax crayons, soft brush, clean cloth.

Permission must be obtained in advance from the vicar. Remove any dirt from the brass with a soft brush. Roll out the paper over the brass, cut it to the required length and fix it down with masking tape, or hold it down with some weights. Rub over the paper with a clean cloth to locate the outline, then rub with the wax as evenly as possible.

Besides the traditional black heel-ball, coloured wax crayons can be used, and also coloured papers.

A batik can be made from a brass rubbing using the method described in section 39.

Figure 72

72   A brass rubbing

65 Coal-hole plate rubbing

Wax crayons or heel-ball, sheets of lining or kitchen paper, stiff brush, masking tape.

Coal-hole plates are usually found in the pavement outside Victorian houses. They are circular cast iron lids covering the hole through which coal is tipped into the cellars below. The designs on the covers vary greatly. Some are very good, but others are weak in design, and they may also be very worn. Choose a good clear design. Clean out any dirt from the crevices in the lid with a brush. Put the paper over the lid. These lids are 305 mm (12 in.) in diameter, so the paper must be wider than this. Stick the edges of the paper down with masking tape. Feel for the shapes through the paper with the fingers. Then rub the wax evenly over the design as for brass rubbing.

Figure 73

73   Coal hole rubbings cut out and arranged on a large sheet of paper

66 Roll-through print

Kitchen paper, ink, inking roller, inking plate.

This technique is similar to rubbing except that an inked roller is used instead of a crayon. Put a small amount of ink on the plate. Roll this out evenly. Run the roller over a spare piece of paper to remove surplus ink. Place the object to be printed under the paper, then put the almost dry roller over the top so that an impression comes through.

Anything which can be rubbed through can also be rolled through. Anything which can be rubbed through with a dark coloured wax can be rubbed through with a light coloured wax and wax resisted.

Figure 74

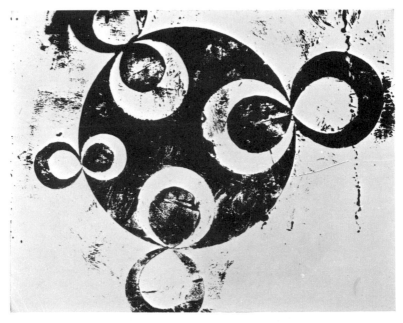

74   Roll-through print using a cut and fold back paper design

Cartridge or stencil paper, craft knife, ink or paint, stencil brush, fixative mouth spray, toothbrush and knife, drawing pins, drawing board.

Cut out the stencil from the middle of the paper. The positive and negative shapes can both be used. Pin the background paper to a drawing board and the stencil to the paper. Rest the drawing board in a vertical position and blow thin paint or ink through the stencil with a fixative mouth spray. Alternatively load an old toothbrush with paint and flick the hairs with a knife blade.

If a stencil brush is used the paper is laid flat on the table. Load the stencil brush with almost dry paint and tap it vertically through the stencil holding the edges of the stencil down with the fingertips of the free hand.

Any flat interesting shapes can be used as stencils such as leaves, pressed flowers, string, wire mesh, keys, scissors, feathers, lace, doylies, fold and cut designs.

Stencils can be used to make a fabric print using fabric printing colours.

Figures 75, 76 and 77

75 *Fire!* Stencil made with a stencil brush and poster paints. Two stencils were used, one for the flames and one for the running figures

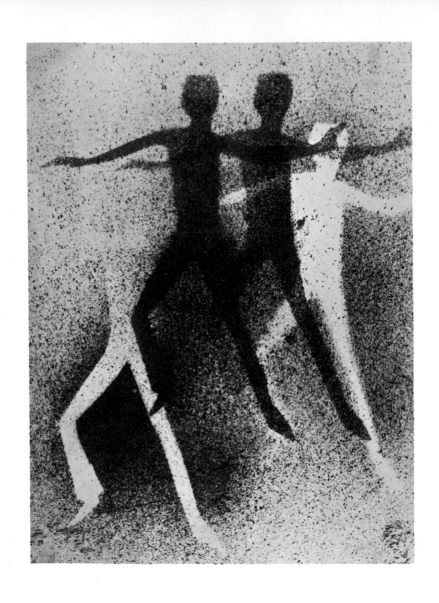

76   Stencil print of dancers. Fixative mouth spray and inks, positive
and negative shapes of a single stencil were used

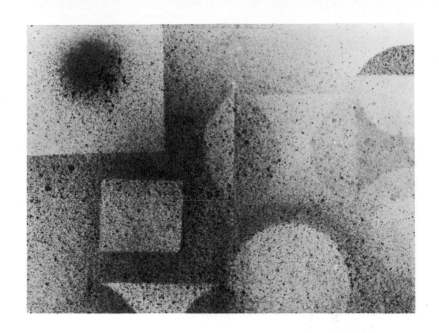

77 Abstract stencil using toothbrush splatter

Photographic paper

68 Dyeline prints

Dyeline paper, dyeline solution, brush, drawing board, sheet of glass.

Put the dyeline paper yellow sensitive side upwards onto a drawing board. Arrange any objects which will create a suitable silhouette on the paper. Do this in a shaded part of the room, or better still in a cupboard with artificial light, then put the board near a window so that daylight or sunlight falls directly upon it. The yellow paper will gradually turn white. How quickly this happens depends on the amount of light available. When the paper is completely white quickly remove the objects and brush dyeline solution over the paper. The silhouette of the various objects will then appear as a permanent print.

If the objects used are very light, such as feathers or leaves, place a sheet of glass over them to prevent any movement.

Dyeline paper deteriorates quickly in store, so it is best to buy only small quantities at a time.

Figures 78 and 79

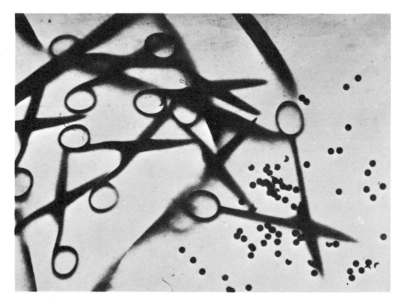

78   Dyeline print of scissors and confetti

79   Dyeline of leaves. The lines of the 'wind' were added afterwards with charcoal

69   Photograms

Darkroom, electric light or photographic enlarger, safe light, photographic paper, dish of developer, dish of fixative, sink for washing prints.

This work must be done in a blacked out room which can be either a proper dark room, a large store, or small room with the window covered over to exclude the light. The light source can be a photographic enlarger or an electric bulb of about 100 watts suspended above a table. A safe light is also necessary so that the operator can see to arrange the objects and to develop and fix the photographic paper.

Place the objects to be printed on the sensitive side of the paper. Arrange these, then switch on the electric light for a few seconds. After switching off, develop, fix and wash the paper.

Figures 80 and 81

80   Photogram: leaves and an electric light flex were placed on the
photographic paper and exposed under an electric light bulb. The
light was switched off, the objects were moved slightly and then the
paper was re-exposed to the light

81   Photogram: two sheets of glass with ink squeezed between them were placed on top of the photographic paper. Leaves, thread and pins were placed on top of the glass

70   Projector slides

Card, *Sellotape* (*Scotch Tape*), scissors, craft knife, inks, liquid detergent. Materials to put into the slides. 35 mm projector and screen or photographic enlarger and developing materials.

Cut two pieces of cardboard each 50 mm (2 in.) square. Cut corresponding windows in these. Collect materials such as dust, seeds, sweet papers, hair, coloured inks, liquid detergent, etc. Sandwich these between two pieces of *Sellotape* and put the *Sellotape* between the cards. Seal the edges of the cards with *Sellotape*. Project onto a screen or put in an enlarger and project onto photographic paper.

Designs can also be painted on glass slides. Cut picture frame glass with a glass cutter into 50 mm (2 in.) squares. Sandwich the materials between the two pieces of glass and seal the edges with *Sellotape*.

Designs can also be made on transparent acetate sheets or rolls and projected from an overhead projector.

These slides can be used to support mime, dance, drama productions by projecting the images onto screens on the stage or upon the performers themselves.

Figure 82

71   Scratched negative slides

Old photographic negatives, needle, craft knife or other sharp point, *Sellotape*, photographic enlarger and photographic developing materials, or slide projector.

Use old unwanted negatives. Scratch a design with a sharp point through the emulsion on the matt side of the negative. Two negatives may be used for each slide. This helps to obscure the original images on the negatives and also gives a three dimensional effect. Place the negatives together with emulsion side inwards and seal the edges with *Sellotape*. To make a slide carrier for 35 mm negatives for use in a slide projector, proceed as for *Projector slides* described in section 70.

Figure 83

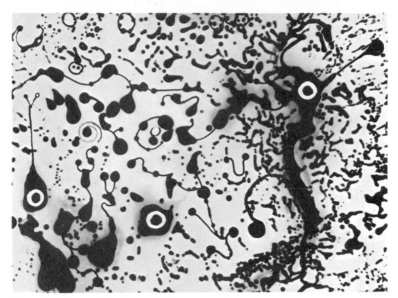

82   Projector slide image printed on photographic paper

83   Scratched negative slide

Collage

Any design partly or entirely made by cutting out and sticking down various materials comes into the category of collage. Its advantages are that it is available to all as a means of expression. It offers great flexibility when designing because the shapes can be moved about into many combinations before being stuck down. The variety of materials used acts as a stimulus to the imagination. It is quick. A design can easily be completed in one art lesson. It is cheap. Most of the materials are scrap such as old newspapers, train tickets, milk bottle tops, magazine illustrations, remnants of cloth, pieces of string, postage stamps, bottle labels, bus tickets.

Figures 84 and 85

84   *Small Bird and the Sun*   Collage: crayon and collage combined. The feathers move in the breeze giving an illusion of movement

85 *Peacock* Collage: the bird is glued to a black cardboard
background. The tail feathers are made of organdie decorated with
milk bottle tops. The body is of thick woollen material. A button is
used for the eye. The flowers are of wool thread

72 String collage

Any sort of string or thread, paper, card or cloth for the background, scissors, adhesive.

Brush adhesive onto one section of the background at a time, put the string into it and bend it to the desired shape. Use the end of a paintbrush if the fingers become too sticky.

Experiment with a variety of strings and thread. They vary greatly in colour, texture and tensile quality, but do not mix too many different strings in one particular work.

Figures 86 and 87

86 *Faces* Wool thread and string

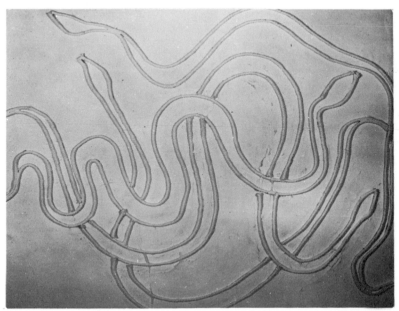

87 *Snakes* String on card painted over with an emulsion paint in one colour

73 Seed collage

Lentils, split peas, gungo beans, millet, rice, maize, sunflower seeds, blackeye beans, macaroni, bean sprout seeds, etc. A strong adhesive, brush, cardboard lid.

Cardboard lids make a useful base as they prevent the seeds from scattering. Sketch the design on the card. Have the seeds ready in separate containers. Glue small areas of the work at a time. Place the seeds on the glue with the fingers or sprinkle them on, then shake and pour off the surplus seeds. Plastic paint can be used to stick the seeds to the background. Seeds of a contrasting colour to the paint can be set in it giving a strong decorative effect.

Figure 88

74 Natural objects collage

PVA emulsion, thick card, scissors, brush.

Collect natural objects of a two dimensional character such as leaves, feathers, flowers, seeds, grasses, insects, seaweed, etc. Arrange the objects on a piece of card. Spread the emulsion over another card of the same size. It must be brushed on thickly leaving no part of the background uncovered. Place the objects into the adhesive in the same order as on the first card, then pour more PVA over them until they are completely covered. Use a brush to get into any awkward places. When first applied, the emulsion will be white and opaque, but will become completely transparent within a few days. The objects treated in this way should retain their natural colour and shape for a very long time.

Figure 89

88   Seed collage

89   Natural objects collage

75 **Paper mosaic**

Old paintings or magazines, scissors, paste, paper.

Cut up old magazine illustrations or old unwanted paintings into small squares. Divide up the squares into basic colours and put each colour into a separate container. Draw out the main areas of the design in pencil. Paste out one small area at a time and stick the pieces firmly on before the paste starts drying. Arrange the squares in vertical and horizontal rows or make them conform to the shapes of the design.

The advantages of magazine illustrations and old paintings over plain coloured papers is that more varied and subtle colours are obtained in this way.

The lesson might be introduced with a talk about the mosaic technique in general and its history.

Figures 90, 91 and 92

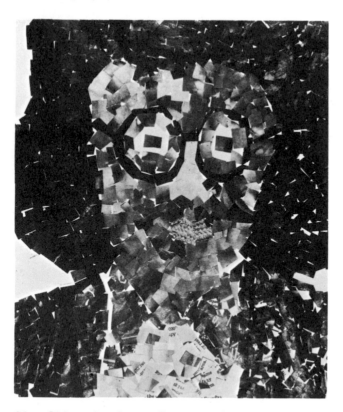

90   *Girl wearing glasses*   Paper mosaic

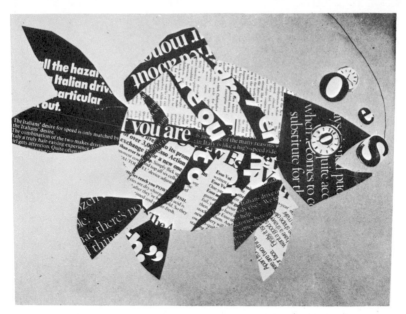

91   *Fish*   Paper collage made entirely of cuttings of type from magazines

92   Arrangement of cut out letters from magazines and spirograph designs. Exercises like these help to make the pupil think of letters and words as designed shapes as well as a means of communication

Photomontage

This is a form of collage made by cutting out, arranging, and pasting down photographs collected from newspapers and magazines. The teacher can suggest a theme, eg cut out and arrange on the background paper as many examples as possible of one object such as bottles, cars, shoes, hands, eyes, ears, mouths, hair, and paste these down, or juxtapose incongruous objects to make pictures similar to those painted by the surrealists. In some cases slots or squares can be cut in the pictures and other cut-out images inserted.

Figures 93 and 94

93   *Eyes*   Photomontage assembled from magazine photographs

94 *Lilliput* A photomontage book illustration. Juxtaposed big and small elements in the design create an illusion of small creatures inhabiting a normal-sized world

Old magazines and newspapers, paper, scissors, paste, *Letraset*.

Young people admire the professional quality of this work, its technical skill, good draughtsmanship and neat lettering, and may feel inadequate when asked to emulate it. Cut-out illustrations and lettering from periodicals can help to overcome their frustration.

Record sleeves   Discuss the qualities in a well-designed record sleeve: suitability of subject, clearness, simplicity and boldness of design. Invent titles or use current commercial successes. Search for suitable illustrations and lettering to fit the titles. It is a good idea to work on more than one sleeve at a time. The designs should be of a standard record size. *Letraset* can be used to supplement the cut-out lettering.

A similar exercise to the record sleeve design can be carried out to produce a book jacket. A visit to the school library preceding the lesson will stimulate ideas and suggest titles. The completed jacket can be cut out of stiff paper and fitted to an actual book to simulate the real thing.

Poster   Discuss the function of the poster, which is to convey a quick clear message using big simple shapes with a striking idea to hold the attention.

Figures 95 and 96

95   *War!*   Photomontage record sleeve

96   A poster. The combination of different letter forms gives vitality
to the design. The humorous approach can often be successful

Folding and cutting paper

77 Split pictures

Magazines or old paintings, scissors, paste, sugar paper.

Cut out photographs from magazines or use old paintings.
Cut these into vertical or horizontal strips. Rearrange these
strips and paste them down side by side to form new pictures.
A repetition is obtained giving an effect similar to an image
in multiple mirrors.

Figure 97

78 Cutting out and folding back

Papers of contrasting colours, scissors, paste, brush.

Cut a large shape from a piece of paper and cut shapes from
its edges. Paste the large shape down on a sheet of paper of
contrasting colour. Paste the small shape down opposite the
openings from which they have been removed.

Figure 98

97 Split picture. An abstract painting cut up and reassembled as described in Section 77

98 Cutting out and folding back. The papers were coloured on one side and white on the reverse. The shapes removed are in each case related in form to the larger parent shape

115

79 Exploding paper designs

Papers of contrasting colours, scissors, paste, brush.

Cut out a basic shape from paper. Start with a simple shape such as a square, circle or triangle. Cut or tear it up into sections, and number these so that they can be kept in their original order. Space them out on another sheet of paper of a contrasting colour and paste them down.

Figures 99 and 100

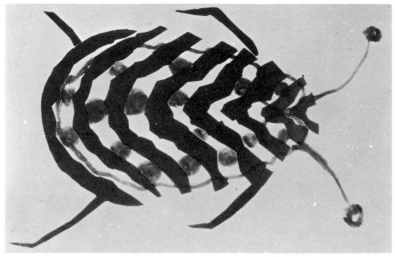

99   *Beetle*   Exploding paper shape. A circle cut out of black paper and spaced out and pasted onto a white background. The result suggested the shape of a beetle so spots, legs and antennae were added

80 Fold and cut paper, snowflake crystals

Coloured papers, scissors, paste, sponge.

Fold a paper square into four, then fold it diagonally. Cut out shapes from the edges. Each shape should be separated from the next by a bridge of paper. Fold and cut other papers of various colours in the same way. Open out and arrange these on a background paper, then paste them down. If gummed papers are used, dampen the backs of the papers with a sponge and use the sponge to press the paper into place.

Figure 101

100   An 'exploded' oblong piece of paper on a contrasting background

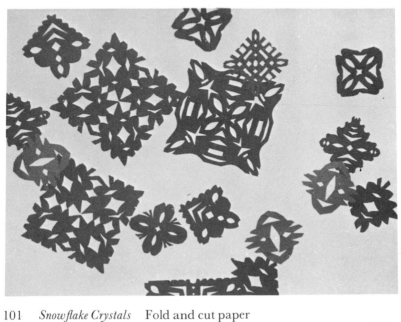

101   *Snowflake Crystals*   Fold and cut paper

81 Tissue paper

Tissue paper, scissors, rubber solution or clear varnish, brush, cartridge paper or tracing paper, *Sellotape* (*Scotch Tape*).

The background paper to which the tissue is attached should be white to give luminosity. For maximum luminosity attach the paper to a window pane. Tissue paper can be fixed down to the background paper with water paste, but the dyes in the tissue paper tend to run. This in itself can be an attractive element, but may not be desired. However, a few spots of rubber solution will suffice to hold the paper. Alternatively, clear varnish can be spread over the background, the tissue placed into it, and another coat of varnish brushed over the top. This gives very brilliant colours, but the composition must be carefully worked out beforehand because it is very difficult to move the papers once they have been varnished.

For the first attempt use uncut sheets of tissue paper. Fold these upon themselves and over each other to form more complex shapes. Follow this by cutting and folding the paper, but without removing any part of the original sheets.

Figures 102, 103 and 104

102   Folded tissue paper design

103   Tissue paper design: cut-out shapes replaced elsewhere to 'echo' the spaces from which they have been removed

104   *Fire of London*   Torn tissue paper design attached to a background of tracing paper with varnish

82   Crumpled tissue paper

Tissue paper, card, paste, brush.

Carry out the design on a stiff card background because, when the work is completed, it will be heavy and will require a firm support. Tear the coloured tissue papers into small pieces and crumple these into balls. Spread paste over one area of the design at a time, and press the balls of tissue paper into it before it dries.

Gradations of tone can be obtained by spacing the balls of paper out, by putting them close together, and by varying their size.

Figure 105

105   *Basket of Flowers*   Crumpled tissue paper

83 Letrafilm

Letrafilm, scissors, craft knife, glass or paper.

This transparent adhesive coloured paper can be attached to any smooth surface and is particularly successful on transparent backgrounds. Draw the design on the back of the paper and cut it out. Peel off the backing paper and press the tacky side onto the background material. If it is attached to glass, further shapes can be cut from the paper with a craft knife after it has been stuck down.

This material can be obtained in matt and gloss finish. It is possible to use inks and paints on the matt papers. The gloss papers can be used to make slides for projection purposes.

As a contrast to the above, experiment with *Letrafilm* on dark backgrounds. This produces very subtle colour effects.

Figure 106

106   *Letrafilm* on windows shows off the material at its best

THREE-DIMENSIONAL WORK
Paper and card

84 Paper relief

Cartridge paper, craft knife, board for cutting on.

Cut openings into the cartridge paper. Bend them outwards or inwards, but do not remove any part of the paper. Reliefs like this depend for their full effect on light and therefore should be placed near a source of light such as a window.

Cartridge paper is a most suitable material to use because it is very flexible, yet sufficiently stiff to support itself, and also, being white, it gives full effect to the shadows. Dark papers are not suitable in this respect.

Figure 107

107   Relief cut in paper. The edges of the paper have been joined to form a cylinder

85 Paper sculpture

Card or cartridge paper, scissors, craft knife, cotton wool, paste, paint.

Many figures and animals can be made by using a cone or cylinder shape as a base, such as angels, birds, insects, mice, pigs, crocodiles, with the addition of paper wings, whiskers, tails, legs, etc.

To make a Father Christmas based on a cone shape roll the paper or card into a tubular shape. Hold one end firmly and allow the other end to expand under its own tension, to form a cone.

Stick the edges together with a strong adhesive. Paint the hat, face and coat, push a piece of cotton wool in the top with some paste on it. Cut paper bands for the bottom of the hat and the bottom of the coat, and attach these. Eyes, moustache, beard, and buttons are cut from separate pieces of paper and pasted on.

Figure 108

86 Card relief covered with foil

Card, craft knife, scissors, silver foil, adhesive or *Sellotape* (*Scotch Tape*), oil paint, brush.

Cut a rectangle from a piece of card. Draw and cut various shapes from another piece of card. Arrange and stick these down on top of each other to make a relief. Cover the top side of the relief with a sheet of foil slightly larger than the rectangle of the card. Gently press the foil into and around the shapes. Fold it under the card and fix the edges down with *Sellotape* or glue. Brush paint over the foil, then rub it off while it is still wet so that it remains in the cracks and indentations.

Figure 109

108   *Father Christmases*   Based on paper cone shapes

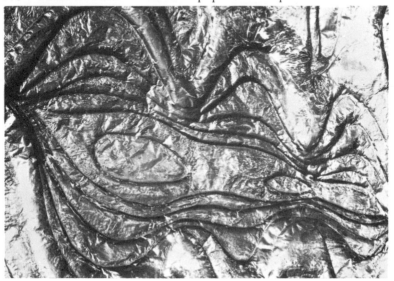

109   Foil-covered card relief

87 Foil modelling

Aluminium cooking foil, scissors, adhesive, clear varnish, oil paint.

To model a figure put several oblong sheets of foil together. Make two cuts at one end and one cut at the other end of the foil. The sections between the cuts will make the arms, head and legs of the figure. Squeeze and twist the paper into shape. When the body is sufficiently formed, concentrate on the action of the figure. If the proportions are incorrect add more foil by wrapping extra sheets around the figure and glue if necessary. If colour is required, add a small amount of oil paint to clear varnish, and paint the figure, but it must be remembered that one of the main attractions of this work is its glittering surface texture.

Many other creatures and shapes can be made along the same lines. Several people can work on one model if it is big enough. This may require the use of several rolls of foil, but other papers can be used for the core of the work.

Figure 110

88 Cardboard sculpture

Cardboard, scissors, craft knife.

Cut the card into rectangular shapes of various sizes. Make a cut in each piece of card. The width of these cuts will depend upon the thickness of the card to be inserted so that it will fit without being too tight or too loose. Slot one card into the next to make a tall structure with the larger cards at the bottom. If the construction is well made it should not need adhesive to hold it together.

Figure 111

126

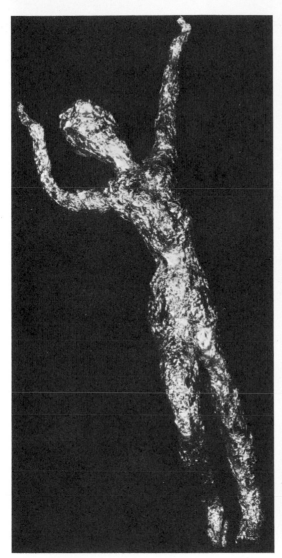 

110   A figure modelled in tinfoil   111   Cardboard sculpture

89　Cardboard tube sculpture

Cardboard tubes of various sizes, craft knife, adhesive.

Join the tubes together to form a sculptured shape with strong adhesive. The ends of the tubes can be cut at different angles, or the tubes can be cut vertically or horizontally into sections. The work can be mounted upon a cardboard or wood base. If the tubes have printed matter on them, the entire work can be painted in one colour to achieve a unity of design.

A similar construction can be made using cardboard boxes of various sizes.

Figure 112

112　Cardboard tube sculpture

90 Mobiles

Any suitable materials, particularly cane, balsa wood, wire, cartridge paper, cardboard, thin tin, straws and cork. Adhesive.

Mobiles must be light and strong and should be able to move freely in a light current of air. Apart from this, they can be made from all sorts of materials, and can be any size, shape or colour.

The mobiles should be suspended high up out harm's way, but not too near to an open window or door where strong draughts may damage them.

Figures 113 and 114

113   *Fish mobile*   The fish were cut from card. The pyramid shapes were made from drinking straws joined at the ends with *Bostik*

114   *Large face mobile*   The middle area of the face was cut out of a large sheet of card. Eyes, nose and mouth were cut from this section. Threads were attached to these with *Bostik* and they were then suspended inside the face. The face is painted on both sides, and when in motion constantly changes expression

91 Drinking straw construction

Drinking straws, scissors, *Bostik*, newspaper.

Cover the tables with newspapers. Join one straw to another by twisting one end into a point and inserting it into the open end of another straw. Alternatively, put blobs of *Bostik* on the ends of the straws. Allow them to become tacky before joining. Keep the sticky parts of the construction away from the table by placing spare straws beneath them. The straws can also be joined by inserting and bending small pieces of pipe cleaner in their ends.

If big projects are attempted, the children can work in teams and parts can be pre-fabricated before being combined into larger units. Straws can be painted, but because of their waxy surface, water-based paints will not adhere well. Very successful mobiles can be built with drinking straws because they are so extremely light. They can be constructed on the same lines as described above.

Figure 115

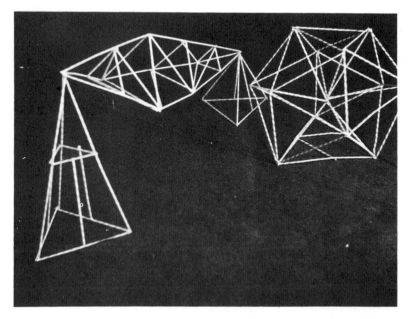

115   Drinking straw construction

Clay

All objects which are made in clay must be fired after drying out to make them permanent, therefore a kiln of some sort is essential. This need not be an expensive object, the cost really depends on the size of the kiln which in turn depends upon the quantity of pottery to be fired. It is possible to make your own kiln, but the heating, usually gas or electricity, should be installed by experts.

Apart from firing, clay pieces can also be glazed, but this is not essential. Glazing can add to the decorative quality of the materials and also help to make the clay impervious to liquid and hygienic. Glazes can be roughly divided into glossy and matt, transparent and opaque, coloured and colourless. The choice of glaze will depend upon the nature of the ware and personal preference. Glazes can be bought ready prepared or can be made up by the potter from basic materials, the latter being the best method in the long run.

For detailed information about kilns, firing and glazes, consult some of the pottery books which deal with this subject, a list of which will be found at the end of this book.

92 Impressed clay tiles

Two sticks of wood approximately 460 mm × 25 mm × 6 mm
(18 in. × 1 in. × ¼ in.). Cloth, rolling pin, ruler, knife.

Put the prepared clay onto a piece of smooth damp cloth with
the sticks on either side. Roll out the clay with a rolling pin
until it is the exact thickness of the sticks. The decoration is
made by pressing objects into the damp clay. Experiment with
a variety of natural and artificial objects such as the ends of
modelling tools, matchsticks, pebbles, screwheads, twigs,
bones, shells, leaves and also the finger ends. Press them firmly
in, and remove cleanly. Afterwards measure out the size of
the tiles and cut them up with a ruler and knife.

Figure 116

116   Tile decorated by pressing parts of kiln furniture into the damp
clay surface

93 Clay tile with pressed linocut relief

Linocut, woodblock, saw, strong adhesive. Clay. Two sticks of wood approximately 460 mm × 25 mm × 6 mm (18 in. × 1 in. × ¼ in.). Cloth, rolling pin, ruler, knife.

Prepare the clay as described in the section on *Impressed clay tiles*. Old well-designed linocuts can be used to decorate the clay tiles. Glue the linocut to a block of wood cut to the same dimensions as itself. Press the lino-block into the clay and withdraw cleanly. The clay should be firm but not too hard, otherwise it will crack.

Figure 117

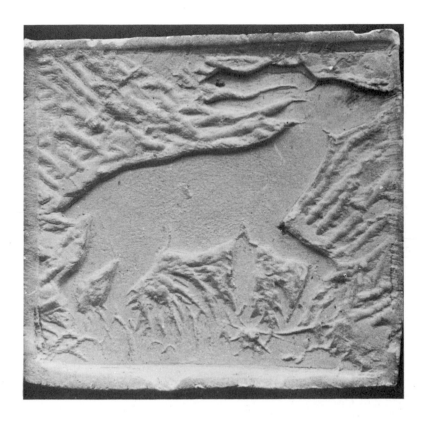

117   Clay tile with pressed linocut relief

94 Clay decorated with engraved plaster cylinder

Cardboard tube or jam jar, plaster, pointed tool for engraving
the cylinder. Clay, two sticks of wood approximately 460 mm
× 25 mm × 6 mm (18 in. × 1 in. × $\frac{1}{4}$ in.), cloth, rolling pin
ruler, knife.

Put an upright cardboard tube on the table top. Surround the
bottom of the tube with clay to prevent liquid plaster from
escaping and to stop the tube from falling over. Mix up the
plaster and pour it into the top of the tube. When the plaster
is set, peel off the cardboard. A jam jar can be used instead
of a cardboard tube. After the plaster has set, wrap the jar in
a piece of cloth and break it gently. Allow the plaster to dry
out, then scratch a design into the surface with a suitable
pointed tool. Prepare the clay as described in section 92.
Wash the cylinder to remove particles of plaster, and roll it
with a firm and even pressure over the prepared clay, then
cut up the clay into separate tiles.

Figure 118

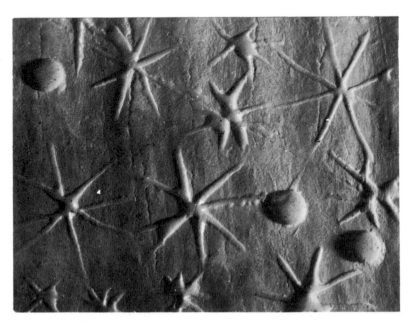

118   Detail of a clay tile decorated with an engraved plaster cylinder

95 Pressed pellets and coils in clay

Two sticks of wood approximately 460 mm × 25 mm × 6 mm
(18 in. × 1 in. × ¼ in.). Cloth, rolling pin, ruler, knife.

Roll up small pellets and coils of clay on the table top. Arrange
these into a design on the surface of the prepared clay tile.
Put a board or card on top, and press them gently into the
surface.

96 Carved decoration

Clay, wire modelling tool, pencil, knife.

Decoration can be carved into the surface of the leather-hard
clay by incising or excising, that is, by lowering the design
and leaving the background raised at its original thickness,
or the reverse, by lowering the background and leaving the
motif or pattern raised. Outline the design with the point of
a pencil. Remove areas of clay with a wire modelling tool or
with a knife blade.

97 Ceramic jewellery

Clay, wire modelling tool, pencil, knife, needle, paper.

Pendants, buttons, brooches, etc, can be made from clay.
Make a preliminary drawing on paper. Allow for clay shrinkage
by making the drawing slightly larger than is required for the
finished article. Roll out a clay slab, trace the drawing onto
the clay by pressing lightly through the paper with a pencil.
Cut the basic shape from the slab with a knife. Allow the clay
to stiffen, then carve a design in the clay with a needle, knife
and modelling tool.

To make beads, roll out an even coil as described in section
99. Cut the coil up into small pieces and roll them in the palms
of the hands. Allow the clay to stiffen, then put a hole through
each bead with a wire. Remember that all shapes and holes
must be made slightly bigger to allow for shrinkage. Biscuit
firing should present no problems, but for glost firing great
care must be taken to see that the glaze on these small objects
does not touch some other objects in the kiln. For bead glazing,
make a rack on the slab pot principle (see section 100) with
holes on opposite sides of the rack to take a number of wires.

Biscuit-fire the rack. String the beads onto wires, and insert these into holes in the rack. Before putting the rack in the kiln, make sure that the beads are well spaced out and that no glaze has got into the holes in the beads.

98   Thumb pots

Clay, modelling tools, knife.

Roll the prepared clay into a ball, hold it in the palm of the hand and push the thumb of the other hand down the centre, but not to the bottom. Squeeze the clay gently between the thumb and fingers. Keep turning all the time while slowly squeezing the sides so that they become thinner and higher. When the pot is the right thickness, which will depend upon its size, trim the top edge with a knife and flatten the base.

99   Coiled pots

Clay, compass, modelling tool, knife.

To make the base of the pot flatten a ball of clay to the required thickness. Mark out the circumference of the base with a compass, and cut it out with a knife. Roll out long pieces of clay on the table with the palms of the hands. The coils must be of even thickness. Place the first coil on the top of the circumference of the base. Cut off the surplus and join the ends by pressing them together and dragging the clay across to seal the gap. Make the second coil slightly longer and place it on top and towards the outer edge of the first to make the sides of the pot go outwards. Continue to build up the wall in this way. Shorten the coils to bring the sides of the pot inwards. If the pot tends to sag, leave it for a while to allow the clay to stiffen. Weld the coils together as the pot rises by dragging clay across from one coil to the next with a modelling tool. If the decorative quality of the coils is desired on the outside, smooth the inside of the pot only.

Figures and animals can also be made by the pinching and coiling methods described.

Figure 119

119   A coiled pot

100 Slab pots

Clay, sticks, rolling pin, damp cloth, knife, ruler, scissors, paper or card for templates, modelling tools, sponge.

Make the slabs for the sides of the pot by rolling out the clay between sticks as for tile making. Cut the sides of the pot out with a ruler and knife. Paper or card templates can be used to obtain matching sides. The clay must be leather-hard before constructing the pot. Scratch the edges of the clay slabs and wet them with slip before joining. For extra strength work thin coils of clay into the inside angles of the pot. Use a modelling tool to weld the joins together inside and out.

Figure 120

101 Slab sculpture

Materials as for slab pots, paper and pencil.

Prepare a clay slab as for making slab pots. Draw a profile pattern of the sculpture on paper. Cut out the drawing and place it on the slab. Cut around this template with a knife to produce two clay shapes for the sides of the sculpture. Use a lump of clay of a suitable shape to support the two halves of the work, then join the halves by nipping them firmly together round the edges. Allow the clay to become leather-hard before removing it from the support. Work over the joins with a modelling tool. If necessary support the work on a thick clay slab base. Coils of clay can be used to support the underneath of the model.

Figure 121

120   Slab pots. The lid of the middle pot has been decorated with inset pieces of glass. The glass was broken into small pieces and set into a cavity in the lid. Tests to obtain the flux temperature of the glass were made beforehand

121   Slab sculpture based on cylindrical shapes made on the same principles as slab pottery

102 Wax resist on pottery

Biscuit fired pottery, underglaze colours, slips and glazes.

Wax can be used to decorate biscuit-fired clay. It is applied in the same way as for paper batik by drawing with wax crayons, or by brushing or dripping wax on the surface of the pottery. Wax can also be applied over large areas with a brush and scratched through with a sharp point. Underglaze colours, slips and glazes are applied by brushing, pouring or dipping. The wax will resist these liquids and, when the pottery is fired, it will be burnt away.

Figure 122

103 Clay modelling

Clay, modelling tools, modelling board, damp cloth, sheet of plastic.

Beginners usually tend to draw on the surface of the clay rather than model it. Press the fingers well into the clay. Bumps and hollows should be strongly emphasized. Hold a ball of clay in one hand, and remove pellets from it with the fingers of the other hand, and press these onto the main mass of the clay. This is the very opposite to carving, where the sculpture is formed by removing material. Refining of shapes can be done with modelling tools, but do not attempt an over-detailed or smooth finish. The over-all form should be compact. Long thin appendages are not suitable to the material, and they break easily.

If the work has to be interrupted before completion it must be kept damp by enclosing it in a damp cloth or plastic sheet, and if possible should be kept in a damp cupboard. If the work is at all large, it should be hollowed out with a wire modelling tool or a spoon, otherwise it may break up when it is fired. Before the work is fired in the kiln, it is necessary to allow it to dry out slowly and thoroughly.

Figures 123 and 124

122   Tile and pot decorated with wax resist

123   Portrait head in kiln-fired clay. If possible a model should be available for this sort of work so that the proportions and shapes of the features can be studied, or the pupils can study each others' features or themselves in a mirror

124   Modelled clay reliefs

Plaster

104 **Plaster modelling**

Plaster, wire or wire netting, newspaper, a wood block, pliers, rag, hammer, staples.

Twist wire or wire netting into the basic shape of the piece of sculpture. If this is not very stable, fix it with staples to a wood base. If a large space is left in the centre of the work, this can be filled with newspapers to reduce the amount of plaster required. Tear up cloth into strips and dip these into thin liquid plaster. Twist and stretch them around the wire frame. Mix a thicker quantity of plaster and trickle this all over the structure, modelling it with the hands where necessary. Certain forms may be accidentally 'found' in the work. These can be accentuated by further modelling or by carving when the plaster has set.

Penknife, surform tools, stone carving chisels, mallet, file, bench with vice or G cramps, wooden box, sand.

To make a plaster block for carving, use a wood or cardboard box. Pour the liquid plaster in and when it has set remove the outside support.

Direct carving can be commenced straight away or the work can be planned as for woodcarving with outline drawings made on the sides of the block. The block can be held by a vice, G cramps, or can be supported in a box of sand.

These materials are easy to carve, but are also very fragile. If mallet and chisels are used, the material should not be struck too hard or the carving may fracture. Elongated shapes should be avoided because they break easily and are difficult to repair. Keep to simple compact forms. If surform tools are used, keep these separate from those used for woodcarving because these materials tend to blunt the tools quickly. When carving irregular shapes such as chalk, the natural shapes of the material can suggest ideas, and these can be developed by deepening and accentuating the forms.

Figure 125

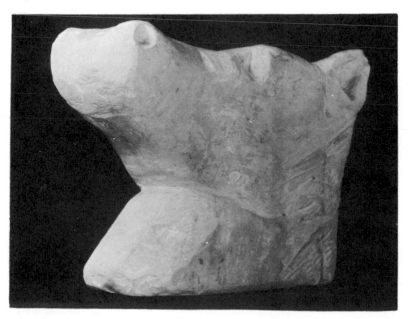

125   Horse's head carved in chalk

Wood and metal

106 Wood relief panel

Round and flat surform tools, coping saw, bench, G cramps or vice, glasspaper.

The wood should be at least one inch thick. Make an outline drawing of the relief on paper. Avoid sharp internal corners to the design. Transfer the drawing by tracing it onto the wood, arranging it so that the minimum of short grain is used. Cut away the waste material around the outline with a coping saw. Round the shapes with the surform tools, and finish off with glasspaper. The work can be polished with linseed oil or furniture wax. If a background is required the carving can be glued to a flat piece of wood.

107 Wood carving

Straight and curved gouges. Mallet, saw, wood-drill, round and flat files, glasspaper, bench with vice or G cramps.

Use fairly hard seasoned wood. Ideas can first be sketched out on paper and modelled in clay or plasticine. Make two outline drawings of two points of view of the carving. Trace off one of the drawings onto opposite sides of the block of wood. Remove large areas of wood around the outlines with a saw, then carve down to the outline with a gouge, cutting with the grain. Trace the other drawing onto the front and back of the block as clearly as is possible on the carved surface. Remove the waste wood as before. Holes and hollows can be developed by using a drill. Now the shapes have to be rounded. Beginners tend to take off too little wood and retain the squareness of the block. Work around each shape and across the grain, keeping the shape to be revealed constantly in mind. The forms should appeal to the sense of touch as well as sight. Do not remove more wood than the chisels can manage at one time, and always keep them very sharp. Obtain a smooth scratch-free finish with medium and fine glasspaper.

Layering Make a block by glueing various planks of wood together and set this in a vice. When the glue has dried, carve the block as described above.

Figure 126

126   *Bud*   Woodcarving

108　Nail relief

Large-headed nails, hammer, thick piece of wood.

Thick blockboard makes a good base as it reduces the risk of the wood splitting. The surface of the wood should be cleaned and polished before putting in the nails. If a preliminary drawing is made on paper, use white chalk on the back of the paper and trace the design off onto the wood surface with a pencil. Put the nails in at different heights and angles to reflect the light like a mosaic. Cloth or a thick newspaper can be put under the wood to help reduce the noise.

Figure 127

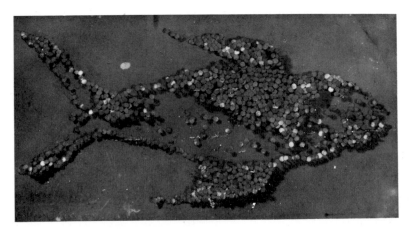

127　*Fish*　Tintacks in blockboard

109 Covered wire sculpture

Soft iron wire, pliers, rag, string, paste, scissors, paint, newspaper, picture varnish.

Twist and bend the wire into the basic shape required. Tear up strips of cloth and bind and tie these around the wire until it is completely covered, then paste several layers of newspaper over the figure. When the paper is completely dry, paint the model with oil or plastic paint or use powder paints and a final coat of varnish.

Figure 128

128   *Giraffe*   Wire covered with rag and newspaper

110 **Wire picture**

Soft iron wire, pliers, hardboard, nails, hammer, solder and soldering iron.

Paint a piece of hardboard in a light colour. Put evenly spaced nails around the edge of the board. Stretch the wire across from nail to nail to make a lattice work. Weave more wire between these to form a design. The wires can be joined by twisting them around each other or, for more permanent work, they can be joined with a soldering iron.

Figure 129

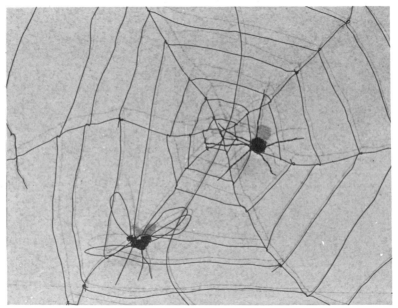

129   Wire picture

111 **Wire sculpture**

Soft iron or galvanized wire, pliers, insulating tape or solder and soldering iron.

The simplest way of joining the wires is by twisting one wire round another, but for stronger joins sticky insulating tape can be used or the joins can be soldered.

Wire sculpture is really like line drawing in space, so it is a good idea to make preliminary drawings in pen and ink on paper. When constructing the work, constantly turn it round to see that it is equally effective from every angle.

Figure 130

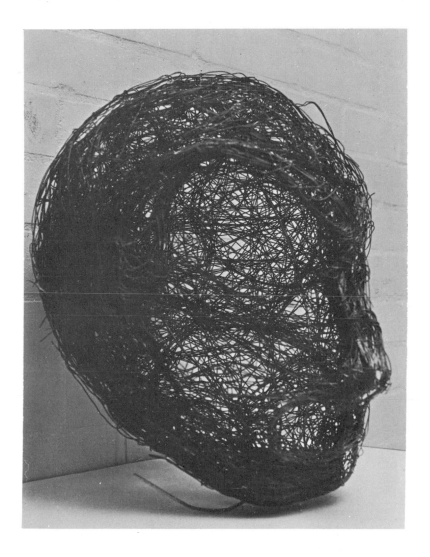

130   Large head made with soft iron binding and copper wire

112   Tin sculpture

Tinplate, tinman's snips, woodblock, nails, hammer.

Tinplate of 0·04 mm thickness is suitable. It can easily be cut by even young children with tinman's snips.

Cut into the metal sheet at various angles, but do not remove any part. Bend and twist these flanges. The cutting process will cause the tin to curl, and this can be accentuated. Make a large flange at the bottom of the work, and nail this to a block of wood to act as a stand. Bend the sculpture this way and that to obtain a good balance.

Figure 131

131   Tin sculpture cut from one sheet of tinplate

113 Punched metal design

Tinplate, tinman's snips, various sizes of nails, hammer, wooden board, file, cloth or newspaper.

Use a fairly thick piece of board to work on because the nails will penetrate the tin and damage the surface beneath. Put several pieces of newspaper or cloth on the board under the tin. Mark out the design by scratching with a sharp point. Punch holes into the metal with a hammer and nails of various thicknesses from one side only. File down the sharp points which are raised around the holes.

Figure 132

132 Tinplate punched with nails of various sizes

Masks and puppets

114 Paper bag mask

Large paper bag, scissors, craft knife, paste, paint, card, raffia.

Put the bag over the head to ascertain and mark the position of the eyes and shoulders. Remove the bag and cut ample arm-holes. Reinforce these round the edges. Eyeholes must also be cut large so that the person wearing the mask can see out clearly. These holes will also serve as ventilators. Nose, ears and mouth can be painted on the bag or made from cardboard and paper, and attached. Hair can be made from straw, raffia, string or curly paper strips.

Smaller paper bags can be used as masks and treated in the same way, but as they will only cover the head an appropriate costume would have to be devised for the actor's body.

Figure 133

133   Paper bag mask

115 Masks

Card, scissors, craft knife, elastic tape, paint, brush.

Hold the card in front of the face and feel for the position of the eyes, nose and mouth. Mark these and cut them out with a craft knife. Draw the outline of the mask on the card and cut it out and paint it. Make two holes on either side of the mask in the middle, and tie a strong elastic tape at the back between them so that it fits just above the ears.

Figure 134

134   Cardboard mask

116 Large paper head

Big and small balloons, newspaper, kitchen paper, card, scissors, craft knife, paste, paints, brushes.

Cover a large inflated balloon with strips of wet paper. Do not use paste on the first layer so that it does not stick to the balloon. Use a different type of paper for alternate layers so that a check can be kept on the thickness of the head. About ten layers of paper will be needed. Do not cover the nozzle of the balloon. The nose and eyes can be made in the same way as the head using smaller balloons. Attach these with pasted strips of paper. Fix cardboard ears in the same way. Allow the head to dry thoroughly, then deflate the balloon and withdraw it through the nozzle hole so that it can be used again. A large hole can be made underneath if the head is to be worn.

Figure 135

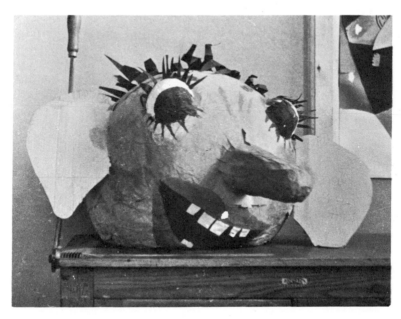

135   Large paper head

117 Shadow puppets

Medium thick card, scissors, craft knife, bicycle wheel spokes, brass paper clips, hammer, pliers.

Shadow puppetry depends for its effect on a shadow being cast by the puppet onto a white screen. A light is projected onto a puppet which is held by the operator close to the screen. The audience sits on the other side of the screen and observes the movements of the shadow, the operator being hidden from view by an opaque curtain or board.

Draw the required shape on the card. Any parts which are to move must be drawn separately. Keep the moving parts to a minimum, otherwise the operator will find the puppet too difficult to handle. When designing the puppet, always think of it as a silhouette. Cut out the shapes with scissors and craft knife. Perforations within the shape which let the light through add to its attractiveness, but they must not weaken the structure. Join the moving parts by piercing small holes at the joints and inserting brass paper clips. The moving parts are controlled with stiff wires. Bicycle wheel spokes are very suitable for this. To attach the end of the wires to the puppet, pierce holes in the card, insert the end of the wires for about 12 mm ($\frac{1}{2}$ in.), then bend the ends over and hammer down. The puppets can be made of black card, can be painted black, or can be decorated with coloured paints. If a coloured shadow is desired, transparent coloured materials such as acetate sheet or gelatine can be used instead of card. Coloured tissue paper can be stretched across the perforations in a cardboard puppet. Coloured lights can be used. This will produce complementary colours in the shadows.

Figure 136

136　*Butterfly*　Shadow puppet

118　Screen and scenery for shadow puppets

A very simple screen can be made by pinning a white sheet across a doorway with a board or an opaque cloth below to hide the operators. To make a permanent screen, construct three wood frames of equal height and hinge them together. The dimensions will depend on the size of the puppets and operators. The middle frame will be twice the width of the side frames. Fill in the side frames and the bottom half of the middle frame with opaque material such as canvas or board. The top half of the middle frame will have a white screen stretched across it. When not in use the screen can be folded up and stored away. If scenery is used it can be cut out in the same way as the puppets. It should be kept at the sides of the screen out of the way of the action of the play, and can be pinned to the frame of the screen with drawing pins.

119 Glove puppet

Clay or plasticine, newspaper, kitchen paper, paste, brush, knife, cartridge paper, pipe cleaners, *Sellotape (Scotch Tape)*, paint, fabric for the costume, needle, thread, scissors.

Model the puppet's head in plasticine or clay. The features must be prominent and deeply modelled so that they show up well at a distance. Cover the plasticine head with torn strips of wet paper. Do not use paste on the first layer so that it does not stick to the head. Use a different type of paper for alternate layers so that a check can be kept on the thickness of the head. When a substantial thickness has been built up, allow the head to dry, then cut it in half with a sharp knife. Cut over the crown of the head and behind the ears so that the join will not be conspicuous. Remove the plasticine or clay and rejoin the two halves with strips of pasted paper. Cut a hole in the bottom of the head and insert a tube of cartridge paper which will fit onto the middle finger. Fix this also with pasted paper. Make tubes for the arms of the puppet in the same way. Make the hands by twisting pipe-cleaners together and covering these with pasted paper. Attach the hands to the outside of the arm tubes by wrapping *Sellotape* around them. Paint the head and hands. Make a simple dress long enough to cover the forearm to the elbow. Cut out two T-shaped pieces of cloth, sew them together around the edges, and sew in the neck and hands of the puppet.

Figure 137

120 Papier mâché head

Newspaper, paste, bowl of water, cartridge paper, two glass marbles.

Tear up newspapers into small pieces, and soak these in a bowl of water. Mix paste with the paper, squeeze out the surplus water and paste, make a tube for the neck from cartridge paper, model the papier mâché round the neck into the form of a head, insert two glass marbles for the eyes. Allow the head to dry completely before painting it.

Figure 138

158

137   A glove puppet   138   A papier mâché head

121 Glove puppet stage

The shadow puppet stage described in *Screen and scenery for shadow puppets* (118) will also serve for glove puppets. Put a string across the back of the stage, and hang a cloth from it to form a backcloth. Simple flat paper scenery can be pinned to this.

Different coloured cloths, soft materials for stuffing, scissors, needle and thread, buttons, pins.

Keep to simple two-dimensional shapes. This avoids using complicated gussets. Draw an outline of the toy on paper. Trace this onto the two pieces of cloth which will form the sides of the toy. Cut the shapes out, then pin them together around the edges. Trim the edges with scissors so that they are exactly the same shape. Use a blanket stitch around the edge leaving a couple of holes through which to push the stuffing. Sew these up when the stuffing has been inserted. Sew on buttons for eyes and other pieces of cloth for ears, fins, etc.

Figure 139

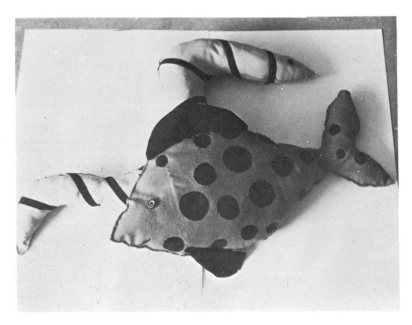

139   Soft toys

Murals and reliefs

123 Polystyrene relief

Polystyrene sheet 25 mm ($\frac{1}{2}$ in.) thick, charcoal, felt tip pen, stiff wire, metal knitting needle or large hatpin, candle or Bunsen burner.

Draw the design on the polystyrene sheet with charcoal or felt tip pen. Specially designed cutters with electrically heated tips can be purchased for cutting polystyrene. However, it can be cut with any hot point such as a metal knitting needle heated in a candle flame or Bunsen burner. The point must be reheated every few minutes in the flame. Plunge the heated needle into the polystyrene, but not quite through it. When complete, the design will show up in an attractive way if it is placed in front of a window so that the light shines through it. It can be backed with coloured papers.

   Of course, if desired, the cutting can be carried right through the sheet so that an open lattice work design is obtained.

Figure 140

140 *Dragon*   Engraving in a polystyrene sheet with a light behind

124 Totem pole

Blocks of expanded polystyrene, saw, sharp knife, hot wire, charcoal, PVA adhesive.

Outline the shapes on the surface of each block with charcoal and cut them out with a saw, knife or heated tool as described in section 123. The shapes should have a family resemblance to each other and should be equally effective from all angles. Many permutations can be made by turning the blocks around. Glue them together when a satisfactory arrangement has been made.

A similar construction can be made by carving woodblocks which can be joined with a simple hole and pin, thus enabling the blocks to be rotated upon each other.

Figure 141

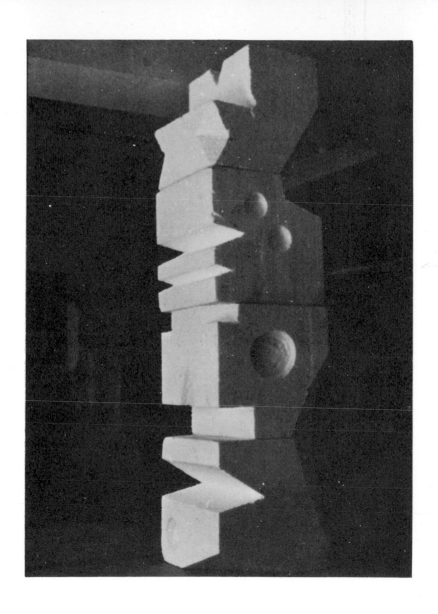

141   Part of a polystyrene totem pole

125 Concrete mural

Concrete, 12 mm ($\frac{1}{2}$ in.) expanded polystyrene sheet, knife, hardboard, nails, hammer charcoal or felt tip pen.

Nail several sheets of expanded polystyrene to a supporting board of the same size. Draw a design on the top sheet of polystyrene with charcoal or felt pen. The shapes are cut out of the polystyrene to varying depths with a sharp knife. Add further nails to any loose areas. The design must be simple and bold, and any thin projections in the mould avoided. When the cutting is completed, nail battens of wood around the mould to contain the concrete. If the mural is large the mould should be lifted to the site before the concrete is poured. Put the face of the polystyrene against the wall so that it forms a box. The top of the mural is left open and the concrete is poured in and vibrated. This can be done with a vibrator, or by hammering the lower part of the box. This vibration causes air bubbles to rise and all cavities to be filled with concrete. When designing the mould it must be remembered that the finished concrete mural will come out in reverse. After the concrete has set the boards and mould are stripped away and the mural cleaned with a stiff brush.

Figures 142 and 143

142　Polystyrene mould for part of a large concrete mural

143　Completed concrete mural with some remains of the mould still attached. The dark areas are the parts of the mural which had already been cleaned with a stiff brush

126 Scrap material mosaic

Wooden frame, clay, plaster, scrap materials: screws, nails, pieces of glass, bottle tops, broken pottery, etc.

To make a two foot square mosaic a frame of wood will be required 610 mm × 102 mm × 13 mm (2 ft × 4 in. × $\frac{1}{2}$ in.) nailed at the corners. Make a bed of clay of an area slightly larger than the frame. Press the frame firmly into this. Press scrap materials face downward into the clay. Remember that the design will come out in reverse. Pour plaster into the box to a depth of 38 mm (1$\frac{1}{2}$ in.). For larger panels, set metal rods into the plaster to support it.

When the plaster has set, remove the frame and clay, and wash the face of the panel.

Figures 144 and 145.

144   *Knight in Armour*   Based on a brass rubbing and made from scrap materials set in plaster. This is about 1·8 m (6 ft) high

145   Detail of the face of the knight

127 Stained glass mosaic

Window or plate glass, small pieces of stained glass, glass cutter, clear *Bostik* or *Epoxy Resin*, white paper, *Polyfilla*, black powder paint.

Scrap glass can be obtained from stained glass studios (usually free). The glass can be used as it comes or, by scoring with a glass-cutter and tapping with a hammer, it can be cut into smaller pieces.

The design is drawn on paper and placed under a large sheet of plain glass. Coloured areas can be indicated on this paper. Plate glass should be used for larger windows, but for smaller panels window glass is adequate. The small pieces of glass are arranged as required, then glued into place with clear *Bostik*. If the window is going outside, a clear epoxy resin must be used as an adhesive. *Polyfilla* mixed with black powder paint is scrubbed into the gaps between the pieces with a stiff brush.

Usually there is more white than coloured glass, in which case better results will be obtained by grouping the colours together and using the white as background.

Make a glass mosaic in plaster using the method described in *Scrap material mosaic* (section 126).

Bibliography

General craft books

Art Techniques for Children, Gottfried Tritten, Batsford London; Van Nostrand Reinhold New York
Creative Crafts for Today, John Portchmouth, Studio Vista London
Creative Crafts, Karl Hils, Batsford London; Van Nostrand Reinhold New York
The Art and Craft Book, Henry Pluckrose, Evans London
150 Techniques in Art, Hans Meyers, Batsford London; Van Nostrand Reinhold New York
150 Themes in Art, Hans Meyers, Batsford London; Van Nostrand Reinhold New York

Basic design

Design Fundamentals, Robert Gillam Scott, McGraw Hill New York
Basic Design, Maurice de Sausmarez, Studio Vista London; Van Nostrand Reinhold New York

Rubbings

Beginner's Guide to Brass Rubbing, Richard J. Busby, Pelham Books London
Brass Rubbing, M. Norris, Studio Vista London; Dover New York
Creative Rubbings, Laye Andrew, Batsford London; Watson-Guptill New York

Collage

Designing with String, Mary Seyd, Batsford London; Watson-Guptill New York
Creative Collage, Ivy Haley, Batsford London; Branford Newton Centre Massachusetts
How to make Collages, John Lynch, Thames and Hudson London
Collage, F. Brow, Pitman London
Creating in Collage, Natalie d'Arbeloff and J. Yates Studio Vista London; Watson-Guptill New York

Curve Stitching and Geometric Shapes

Experiments in Mathematics, J. F. F. Pearcy and K. Lewis Longmans Green London

Drawing and Painting

Introducing Finger Painting, Guy Scott, Batsford London; Van Nostrand Rheinhold New York

Creative Drawing: Point and Line, Ernst Röttger and Dieter Klante Batsford London; Van Nostrand Reinhold New York

Introducing to Crayon Techniques, Henry Pluckrose, Batsford London; Watson-Guptill New York

Pictures with Crayons, Lothar Kampmann, Batsford London; Van Nostrand Reinhold New York

Introducing Acrylic Painting, Henry Pluckrose, Batsford London; Watson-Guptill New York

Acrylics, J. Mills, Pitman London

Painters' Pocket Book of Methods and Materials, Hillier Hiler, Faber and Faber London; Watson-Guptill New York

The Materials of the Artist and Their Use in Painting, Max Doerner, Hart-Davis London; Harcourt Brace New York

Drawing on Scraperboard, Edward S. Billin, Pitman London

Fabric

Colour and Texture in Creative Textile Craft, Rolf Hartung, Batsford London; Van Nostrand Reinhold New York

Introducing Screen Printing, Anthony Kinsey, Batsford London; Watson-Guptill New York (out of print)

Introducing Batik, Evelyn Samuel, Batsford London; Watson-Guptill New York

Batik Fabrics, J. Hobson, Dryad Leicester

Tie and Dye, Ann Maile, Mills and Boon London

Dyed and Printed Fabrics, J. Hobson, Dryad Leicester

Textile Printing and Dyeing, Nora Proud, Batsford London; Van Nostrand Reinhold New York (out of print)

Creative Textile Craft: Thread and Fabric, Rolf Hartung, Batsford London; Van Nostrand Reinhold New York

Mosaics

Making Mosaics, Arvois, Oak Tree Press London
Mosaics, R. Williamson, Crosby Lockwood London

Paper Crafts

Creative Paper Crafts in Color, Chester J. Alkema, Oak Tree London; Sterling New York
Creative Papercraft, Ernst Röttger, Batsford London; Van Nostrand Reinhold New York
Papercraft, D. Meilach, Pitman London
Modelling with Foil, John Milsome, Queen Anne Press London
Creating with Paper, P. Johnson, Kaye London; University of Washington Press
Pictures with Coloured Paper, Lothar Kampmann, Batsford London; Van Nostrand Reinhold New York

Perspective

Perspective, Gwen White, Batsford London
How to draw Perspectives to Scale, W. H. Fuller, Studio London
A Practical Guide to Perspective, G. M. Norden, Pitman London

Pottery

The Practical Pottery Book, Herbert H. Sanders, Blandford London
Pottery without a Wheel, K. Tyler, Dryad Leicester
Beginners' Book of Pottery, H. Powell, Blandford London; Emerson New York
Technique of Pottery, Dora Billington, Batsford London; Hearthside New York
Understanding Pottery Glazes, D. Green, Faber and Faber London and New York
Creative Clay Craft, Ernst Röttger, Batsford London; Van Nostrand Reinhold New York

Printmaking

Creative Printmaking, Peter Green, Batsford London; Watson-Guptill New York (out of print)
Introducing Linocuts, Jane Elam, Batsford London; Watson-Guptill New York
Introducing Surface Printing, Peter Green, Batsford London; Watson-Guptill New York
Linocut and Woodcuts, Michael Rothenstein, Studio Vista London
Making Colour Prints, J. Newick, Dryad Leicester

171

Printmaking, D. Meilach, Pitman London
Introducing Woodcuts, Gerald Wood, Batsford London; Watson-Guptill New York

Puppetry

Shadow Puppets, Olive Blackham, Barrie and Rockliff London
Introducing Puppetry, Peter Fraser, Batsford London; Watson-Guptill New York
Hand and String Puppets, W. Lancaster, Dryad Leicester
Book of Puppetry, Bufano, Collier Macmillan London
Puppetry in the Primary School, D. Currell, Batsford London

Sculpture

Sculpture for Beginners, Maria and Louis DiValentin, Oak Tree London; Sterling New York
Creative Woodcraft, Ernst Röttger, Batsford London; Van Nostrand Reinhold New York
Whittling and Woodcarving, E. J. Tangerman, Constable London; Dover New York
The Carver's Companion, Peter Morton, A. & C. Black London
Creative Light Woodcarving, J. Matthews, Edward Arnold London
Creative Metal Craft, Heinz Ullrich and Dieter Klante, Batsford London; Van Nostrand Reinhold New York
Simple Wire Sculpture, Elizabeth Gallop, Studio Vista London; Watson-Guptill New York

Toymaking

Soft Toy Making, P. Chappell, Evans London
Introducing Soft Toy Making, D. Davidson, Batsford London; Praeger New York
Making Felt Toys, Suzy Ives, Batsford London; Branford Massachusetts

Suppliers of materials   GB

Art supplies, general

Fred Aldous, The Handicrafts Centre, 37 Lever Street, Manchester 76O 1UX

Arts and Crafts, 10 Byram Street, Huddersfield HD1 1DA

Crafts Unlimited, 21 Macklin Street, London WC2

Dryad Limited, Northgates, Leicester

Educational Supply Association, Pinnacles, Harlow, Essex

E. J. Arnold and Company, Butterley Street, Leeds, Yorkshire

Margros Limited, Monument Way West, Woking, Surrey

Clifford Milburn Limited, 54 Fleet Street, London EC4

Nottingham Handcraft Company, Melton Road, West Bridgford, Nottingham (School Suppliers)

Reeves and Sons Limited, Lincoln Road, Enfield, Middlesex

George Rowney and Company Limited, 10 Percy Street, London W1

Winsor and Newton Limited (who also supply ENSINK LITHO sketch materials and PRINTEX (TINOLITE) Pigment colour), Wealdstone, Harrow, Middlesex

Adhesives

Epoxy resin glue, POLYCELL, DUFIX, COPYDEX, GLOY, BOSTIK, UHU all obtainable from the majority of stationers, department stores and do-it-yourself stores. Detailed information obtainable from the relevant companies.

PUA MARVIN MEDIUM, Margros Limited, Monument Way West, Woking, Surrey

EPOXY RESIN GLUE, CIBA Limited, Duxford, Cambridge

POLYCELL, John Lines, Tottenham Court Road, London, W1

DUFIX, Adhesive Sales Department, ICI Limited, Wexham Road, Slough, Bucks

COPYDEX, 1 Torquay Street, London, W2

GLOY MULTIGLUE, Gloy Schools Service, Associated Adhesives Limited, Eighth Avenue Works, Manor Park, London, E12

CLEAR BOSTIK No 1, Bostik Limited, United Marketing, Leicester

Candles and batik supplies

Candle Kit, 8 Oldbury Close, Spring Lane, Ightham, Kent

Candlemakers Supplies, Beaconsfield Terrace Road, London W14

Price's Candle Distributors Limited, 87 South Lambert Road, London, SW8

Dyes

HELIZARIN
Brico Commercial Chemical Company Limited, 55-57 Glengall Road, London, SE15
Comak Chemicals Limited, Department MCG/P Swinton Works, Moon Street, London N1
Polyprint, 815 Lisburn Road, Belfast
DYLON and PROCION
Mayborne Products Limited, 139-147 Sydenham Road, London SE26

Graphic supplies

Davis (Patents) Limited, 18 Phipp Street, London EC2
Gestetner Duplicators Limited, 210 Euston Road, London NW1
Letraset Limited, St George's House, 195-203 Waterloo Road, London SE1
Sericol Group, 24 Parsons Green Lane, London SW6
Selectasine Silk Screen Limited, 22 Bulstrode Street, London SW6

Paper

Spicer-Cowan Limited, 19 New Bridge Street, London EC4 and 19 Dublin Street, Edinburgh EH1 3PG

Paper, coloured and tissue

F. G. Kettle, 127 High Holborn, London WC1
Paperchase Products Limited, 216 Tottenham Court Road, London W1

Photographic equipment

Kodak Limited, 246 High Holborn, London WC1 and branches

Polystyrene

Do-it-yourself and department stores

Pottery

The Fulham Pottery and Cheavin Filter Company Limited, 210 New Kings Road, Fulham, London SW6
Podmore and Sons Limited, Shelton, Stoke-on-Trent, Staffordshire

Wengers Limited, Etruria, Stoke-on-Trent, Staffordshire
ST4 7BQ

Sculpture, general

Alec Tiranti Limited, 21 Goodge Place, London W1 and
70 High Street, Theale, Berkshire

Straws

Artstraws Limited, College Road, Fishponds, Bristol BSI6 2HR

Suppliers of materials   USA

Art supplies, general

The Morilla Company Inc, 43 Twenty First Street, Long Island
City, New York and 2866 West Seventh Street, Los Angeles,
California
Stafford-Reeves Inc, 626 Greenwich Street, New York 10014

Adhesives

Marvin Medium
Eagle Pencil Company, Danbury, Connecticut
Elmer's glue, Sobo
Available from most department stores

Candles and batik supplies

Norman Ceramics Co Inc, 252 Mamaroneck Avenue, Mamaroneck,
New York
Craftool Dyes for Batik, Wood-Ridge, New Jersey 07075

Dyes

Craftool Dyes for Batik, Wood-Ridge, New Jersey 07075
Cushing and Company, Dover Foxcroft, Maine 04426
Stein, Hall and Company, 285 Madison Avenue, New York
Screen Process Supplies Manufacturing Company, 1199 East twelfth
Street, Oakland 6, California
Geigy Chemical Company, PO Box 430, Yonkers, New York

Sculpture, general

Sculpture House, 38 East Thirtieth Street, New York
Commercial Paste Company, 925 West Henderson Road, Columbus, Ohio

Pottery, general

Stewart Clay Co Inc, 133 Mulberry Street, New York 10013
Newton Potter's Supply Inc, 96 Rumford Avenue, West Newton, Massachusetts 02165
Duncan Ceramic Products Inc, PO Box 7827, Fresno, California 93727
Bell Ceramics Inc, PO Box 697, Clermont, Florida 32711

Suppliers of materials   Australia

Reeves (Aust) Pty Ltd, 6 King Street, Balmain, New South Wales 2041
Swain & Co Pty Ltd, 330 George Street, Sydney, New South Wales 2000
Tyrrell's Book Shop Pty Ltd, 328 Pacific Highway, Crows Nest, New South Wales 2065

Camden Art Centre Pty Ltd, 188 Gertrude Street, Fitzroy, Victoria 3065
W & G Dean Pty Ltd, 346 Little Collins Street, Melbourne, Victoria 3000

Abbey Bookshop, 589 Logan Road, Greenslopes, Queensland 4120
Barkers Bookstore, 196 Edward Street, Brisbane, Queensland 4000

Birchalls Pty Ltd, 118 Brisbane Street, Launceston, Tasmania 7000
OBM Pty Ltd, 36 Elizabeth Street and 96 Collins Street, Hobart, Tasmania 7000

S A Art and School Supplies, 40 O'Connell Street, North Adelaide, South Australia 5006

Lansart Supplies, 329 Murray Street, Perth, Western Australia 6000